How Markets Work

Dedicated with Love to:
Falguni A. Sheth

How Markets Work

Supply, Demand and the 'Real World'

Robert E. Prasch

Associate Professor of Economics, Middlebury College, USA

Edward Elgar

Cheltenham, UK • Northampton, MA, USA

Published by
Edward Elgar Publishing Limited
The Lypiatts
15 Lansdown Road
Cheltenham
Glos GL50 2JA
UK

Edward Elgar Publishing, Inc.
William Pratt House
9 Dewey Court
Northampton, Massachusetts 01060
USA

A catalogue record for this book
is available from the British Library

Library of Congress Cataloging in Publication Data

Prasch, Robert E., 1958–
    How markets work : supply, demand and the 'real world' / Robert E. Prasch.
        p. cm.
    Includes bibliographical references and index.
    1. Capitalism. 2. Free enterprise. 3. Markets. I. Title.
    HB501.P69185 2008
    338.5′21—dc22

                                                            2007049440

ISBN 978 1 84720 613 8 (cased)
ISBN 978 1 84720 614 5 (paperback)

Mixed Sources
Product group from well-managed
forests and other controlled sources
www.fsc.org Cert no. SA-COC-1565
© 1996 Forest Stewardship Council
FSC

Printed and bound in Great Britain
by MPG Books Group, UK

Contents

Contents

Acknowledgements

The following lectures have several sources. The most important, although not always voluntary contributors, were the approximately 2000 Introductory Economics students whom I have been privileged to teach at San Francisco State University, the University of Maine, Vassar College, and now Middlebury College. I would like to thank all of them for their patience and even interest as I developed my ideas and pedagogy over the years. Particularly worthy of thanks are my Economics 150 classes from the Fall of 2006 and 2007, who read many of these chapters in an earlier form. All of my students, but especially those from these last two fall semesters, have been an essential guide to what "works" pedagogically, and they have made a material contribution to this book. I would like to thank those students who heard the first lecture when I had occasion to present it at one of my several *alma maters*, the University of Denver, in Spring 2000. I wish to thank two of my former professors, Tracy Mott and David P. Levine, for that opportunity in addition to their inspiration and support over many years.

With hindsight, it is evident that I was the beneficiary of multiple sources of inspiration as I worked through the ideas presented in this book. One was a short paper that Professor Anne Mayhew encouraged, and saw fit to publish, many years ago (Prasch, 1992). While grievously mistitled, it represented an early effort to consider the structures that distinguished one market from another. While I did not know it at the time, Anne recognized that I was rediscovering what serious thinkers within the American Institutionalist tradition had previously understood. This is the proposition that not all markets could or should be "modeled" on the basis of a narrow set of abstract presuppositions and presumptively eternal verities. Later, once I had done a lot more reading and thinking, I came to learn what she already understood, which enabled me to complete several more extended papers on the unique attributes of labor markets. I am grateful to Anne Mayhew along with Professors Lonnie Golden, Deborah Figart, Janet Knoedler, and Dell Champlin for soliciting, encouraging, and publishing this work (Prasch 2000a, 2000b, 2004b). Readers of those papers will readily identify some of those ideas represented in this book.

Several institutions have supported this book. Foundations have not been among them. I am most grateful to my current employer, Middlebury College, for providing me with two leaves, one at a little over half pay for the academic year 2004–2005, in addition to an unpaid leave for the Spring of 2007. These have greatly facilitated the finishing of this work. After over 17 years of uninterrupted college teaching across several institutions, these leaves were a wonderful and welcome opportunity, to say nothing of a needed respite. I would like to especially thank Middlebury Provost and Executive Vice President Alison Byerly for granting those leaves. Additionally, I would like to thank Professor Michael Reich of another of my *alma maters*, U.C. Berkeley, for sponsoring my stay as a Visiting Scholar at the Institute for Industrial Relations for the Spring and Summer of 2007. This visit was most useful, and it greatly accelerated my progress on several projects, including this one. I also wish to thank my colleagues at Middlebury College, especially David Colander and Sunder Ramaswamy, for recruiting and encouraging a colleague whose ideas are so at variance with current professional trends. Each of them embodies the vision and ideals implied by the phase "liberal arts," and for this reason are a credit to the college and themselves.

A number of friends, family, and colleagues have contributed to this book by reading over one or more chapters, perhaps in an earlier format, or in the course of conversations about some of its ideas. Despite my trepidation that any list will inevitably overlook some friends and colleagues, I wish to especially thank Anne Mayhew, Deborah Figart, Lonnie Golden, John Garber, Dell Champlin, Janet Knoedler, Tracy Mott, David P. Levine, Michael R. Montgomery, Oren Levin-Waldman, Jeffrey Carpenter, Peter Matthews, Thierry Warin, Liz Lyon, David Colander, Kevin McCarron, William Steele, Anita Balachandra, Uma Narayan, James K. Galbraith, Mark Lutz, Sandy Thompson, Rebecca Edwards, Pinar Batur, and Bill Lunt for their willingness to read, hear, and discuss various elements and aspects of this book as its ideas were formulated and reformulated over so many years.

Additionally, I would be remiss if I failed to thank the staffs of several cafés who so graciously, if unknowingly, supplied me with tranquillity, coffee, beer and wine as this book was reedited more times than I care to remember. These include Uncommon Grounds and Muddy Waters of Burlington, Vermont; Rao's of Amherst, Massachusetts; Le Royal Jussieu of Paris; and several San Francisco cafés including the Café de Soleil, Being There, Jumpin' Java, iCafe, Kaleo, and the sorely-missed Canvas.

Finally, my deepest thanks and love are due to my sister Sandra, and her family John, Alison, and Sophie Garber, for their kindness and for always providing me with a place to have fun. For the same reason, I am also in debt to my parents, Carolyn and Robert E. Prasch of Grand Isle, Vermont, for their long-standing love, patience, and support, in addition to providing me with that all-important and periodically essential "weekend writing nook" for quiet contemplation and writing.

Another source of support came from an invisible community without a formal name or identity. This is all the wonderful people who continue to insist, despite the scorn of accepted and acceptable opinion, that "Another World is Possible." Knowing that a lot of people do not think that were are at "The End of History" is a thought, and during some dark times perhaps the only thought, that has sustained my hope and effort over these past several decades. Thank you for that.

Ultimately, the most important contributor to this book is the one who has been a continuous source of support and inspiration. Her reward has been to travel with me along a path that was longer and more demanding than either of us imagined. But her unstinting love, support, and willingness to endure trying times has enabled me to retain a portion of my intellectual, emotional, and moral capacity while continuing to work in an academic field that has little use for discussions of its own history or fundamental preconceptions. Her contribution, in other words, goes well beyond her several readings of various portions of the manuscript or our innumerable discussions of all of the ideas presented in these lectures. It even goes beyond her always-essential expertise on computer and printer technology, to say nothing of the English language. Dante was blessed to be guided by Beatrice, but I cannot believe that she provided more inspiration than the person to whom I owe so much and to whom this book is dedicated. Thank you Tina.

PART I

The theory of markets

INTRODUCTION

Economics today: is market fundamentalism in decline?

Since the late 1970s American economic policy has been almost exclusively informed by what Nobel Laureate Joseph Stiglitz has labeled "market fundamentalism" (Stiglitz 2002, 2004). For a remarkable range of issues, from social security to education, public transportation, communications, electricity, water, and the provisioning of other necessities, the "conventional wisdom" has been to aggressively promote deregulation and privatization. This attitude has even spread to quintessential state functions such as the staffing of prisons and even military occupations.

The underlying ideology, one that is now pervasive, is that an unregulated private sector, operating through the legendary "invisible hand," is the only way to meet individual, community, and national needs. As recently as the 1970s such views were exclusively those of a rightist fringe. Things have changed. Today these views are what Washington-based journalists and the sundry "experts" they favor in their news stories and broadcasts call "centrist" or "bi-partisan." With such endorsements, these ideas have been rechristened as the default position for all "responsible" and thereby "worthy" policy commentary. As Stiglitz and others have noted, these narratives have been especially dominant in the sphere of international economic policy.

Parallel to this remarkable political and rhetorical shift, market fundamentalist views have also become the "default" position of the economics textbooks of our nation's colleges and high schools. While these books may set a few pages aside for the tepid presentation of a counterpoint, the overwhelming ethos is to affirm and reaffirm the position that free markets are the strongly preferred approach to resolving economic, and more than a few non-economic, issues.

Living in the center of these trends, today's economists may not have noticed these changes, but by any "external" vantage point it is stating the obvious to comment that in today's economics textbooks balance, nuance, and respectful attention to counter-arguments, are marked by their absence.[1]

In conversation, many professional economists have reminded me that while these trends are indeed present, they have never been hegemonic in the realm of pure economic theory. Neither have they been as hegemonic in the policy discussions of the "higher learning" as exemplified in the profession's academic journals. Of course, such observations are contestable. But however such a discussion might play out, it remains evident that professional economists strongly favor market provisioning as the "default" position for a wide variety of issues, and that their view is in contrast to that of much of the rest of humanity.

Anticipating some objections to the previous paragraph, I wish to immediately affirm that yes, even as the profession was approaching its apex of "market fundamentalist" modes of thinking – around the mid-1980s – dissenting views were represented in the citadels of the higher learning. Additionally, some of the work now routinely invoked to criticize simple-minded applications of the venerable "theory of perfect competition" were then being developed and discussed. Game theory, the economics of information, chaos theory, and experimental economics were each getting some attention by the mid-1980s, although they were then peripheral to the "core" curriculum presented to graduate students. Happily, since the late 1980s, professional economists have expanded the scope of what constitutes accepted and acceptable modes of theorizing. Today, economists remain opposed to the "anything goes" approach to science once promoted by the late Berkeley philosopher Paul Feyerabend. But it is also evident that the theory of perfect competition no longer retains unquestioned dominance over the journal literature or the education of graduate students.

Despite these trends, market fundamentalism remains the perspective of virtually every introductory economics textbook. The reasons for this will not be explored here as this introduction is not the place to initiate a sociology of the economics profession – although such a study is clearly long overdue. What does need to be noted is that despite the confidence of market fundamentalists in the validity of their favored theories and policies, most of the world's citizens remain unconvinced. Indeed, when non-economists make the sustained effort required to understand their writings, they are often surprised by the thinness of the arguments invoked to condemn popular and long-standing public policies. Minimum wage laws, usury laws, truth-in-advertising laws, laws to regulate fraud, health-and-safety codes, anti-discrimination laws, building inspection codes, environmental laws, investor protection rules, and many other rules and regulations have each and severally been breezily, even haughtily, dismissed by market fundamentalists and the many columnists and politicians who invoke their arguments. In all likelihood, the refusal of market fundamentalists to be informed by evidence and experience would embarrass Dr. Pangloss. Experience, intuition, and ethical considerations inform most thinking people that, in the absence of social institutions acting as a check on private property and market forces, we will be treated to a hard lesson. As only he can, Mark Twain described the most likely form that this lesson will take, "The man who carries a cat by the tail learns something that can be learned in no other way."

And these lessons are indeed being learned. Over the last five years and across the world people are electing and reelecting leaders, even some leaders with clear flaws, largely on the strength of their promises to roll back the internationalist incarnation of market fundamentalism – termed "free markets" or "free trade" in the United States, but "Neoliberalism" or the "Washington Consensus" across most of the rest of the planet.[2] Nations as diverse as Argentina and Malaysia are showing the world that countries that check or even roll back the nostrums of market fundamentalism will be rewarded with enhanced economic performance. A particularly instructive and important example is China, which has ignored virtually every policy recommendation of the Washington Consensus. Yet its experience is reaffirming what the economic histories of Japan, the Republic of Korea, and Taiwan (to say nothing of the United States or Germany) have previously demonstrated, that *laissez faire* is not the formula for prosperity.

In light of the above trends, it is apparent that new and revised expositions of elementary economics are required. Such a revision must feature an approach that is more accurate, substantive, and thereby "real world" than that of the current crop of textbooks. For this reason it is my hope that this book will be of assistance to those teachers of economics wishing to present a more balanced course to their students. To this end, it takes a forceful position in opposition to that of the textbooks and the policies of the Washington Consensus in order to provide a clear counterpoint. As in my own classes, it is to be hoped that students will consider all the options and formulate their own views on the basis of the merits of the arguments presented. My additional hope is that these lectures will also be accessible to interested persons in other fields, including the general reader.

A THEORY OF MARKETS, NOT OF "THE MARKET"

The dominant theme of the following lectures – what in my classes I describe as "the story behind the story" – is that there is no single "theory of the market." The widely believed and, in my view, erroneous proposition that there is *only* a single theory of the market is the core misunderstanding and failure of the received approach to economics instruction and policy-making. As such, it follows that any revised exposition of economics must begin by liberating our minds from such a flawed proposition. Thus freed, we will be able to take the crucial first step in abandoning the intellectual biases and blindness of market fundamentalism and its disastrous policies.

By contrast to the error identified in the previous paragraph, the following lectures will recast the elements of economic theory from the perspective that there are several theories of markets. Each theory is thought to have its own realm and scope of applicability. This alternative premise can, I believe, be the basis of a coherent foundation of the elements of economics, while providing a contrast to the received vision.

The following lectures, then, encompass two distinct but related tasks. The first is to present an alternative introduction to the elements of economic theory. A second is to present the basis for a critique of the market fundamentalist perspective. But, I must include a qualification. What follows is not a comprehensive treatise or handbook on economic theory or policy. These lectures do not present and defend a laundry list of specific policies and programs. Rather, the idea is to present the foundation of several theories that can be applied to several types of markets. These lectures might best be taken as guidelines or suggestive avenues of thought for further inquiry into the several markets presented in addition to other markets that may closely conform to one or more of them, or have different properties altogether.

In developing a critique and reconstruction of elementary economics the following lectures will, through a reinterpretation and reframing of the venerable theory of supply and demand, demonstrate that much of what today passes for "economic theory" – specifically as it is now packaged and transmitted to initiates – is not only over-simplified, it is in fact simplistic. As a consequence of being simplistic, much of the received theory is misleading and sometimes even detrimental to the economic prospects of our communities, our nation, and our world. It will be demonstrated that when more plausible assumptions concerning the actual behavioral and structural conditions underlying several important varieties of markets are introduced, the only defensible conclusion is that there are *theories* (plural) of the behavior of *markets* (also plural).

A METHODOLOGICAL INTERLUDE

Before starting it will be prudent to ward off some simple misunderstandings by presenting a brief methodological caveat. First, when I state that there are several types of markets, each with a theory most suited to it, *I am not making* the trivial claim that each market is different in the sense that there are details of fact or circumstance unique to each. In its form and content, broccoli clearly has properties that distinguish it from an automobile, a corporate bond, a designer handbag, or manual labor. This is understood, but it is most emphatically not my point.

Second, *I am not making* the trivial claim that abstraction is an illegitimate activity. Abstraction from the inessential aspects of any problem is a necessary first step to all theorizing: natural, social scientific, philosophical, or literary. If I wish to count the number of coins in my pocket, I can with confidence abstract from knowing which of them are quarters, dimes, nickels or pennies. To learn whether or not these same coins will purchase a subway ticket, the previous abstraction would impede our understanding. In each of these examples, the question is an important consideration in establishing an appropriate abstraction. A similar claim can be made for the theory of markets.

As will be evident, it is my view that our understanding of markets can be improved through the development and analysis of what I will term, following Max Weber, "ideal types." Readers will find that each of the ideal types of markets developed here shares many, even most, of the qualities of the others. Yet, as will be seen, each ideal type also features an idiosyncratic quality of decisive importance for analysis, understanding, and policy evaluation. While parallels and analogies can be made across several of these ideal types, substantive differences remain. As will be seen, these distinctions and similarities have critical consequences for each particular market, and the theories and policies that most plausibly flow from the analysis. Teachers of economics, particularly those over the age of 50, will immediately recognize that my suggested approach is strongly at variance with the views once advanced by the late Milton Friedman (Friedman, 1953).

OVERVIEW OF THE BOOK

By time-honored convention, expositions of elementary economics begin with a hypothetical exchange between two abstract persons in an abstract setting. Soon thereafter, the reader encounters sweeping generalizations concerning the causes of exchange, the theory of demand and supply, the nature and meaning of economic activity, and multiple ungrounded remarks on the futility of well-meaning interventions in markets. Collectively, these lessons are presented as "The Law of Markets." Not covered by such an analysis is any insight into what may be legitimately exchanged, or the rules under which such articles may be exchanged.

This was not always the case. A hundred years ago the teaching of economics, especially in the United States and Germany, began with a discussion of property and contract law. This book will return to this eclipsed pedagogical tradition. The reason is that a sketch of the rudiments of the law of property and contract provides readers with a sense of how the economy is embedded in a set of institutions and norms, rules that may even come to be codified in the laws. For far too long economists, and especially teachers of elementary economics, have simply assumed that a stable and legal framework of markets has been fully worked out. This presumption devalues the importance of these rules and their critical role in managing, stabilizing, and legitimating market exchanges. Either intentionally or inadvertently, long-standing pedagogical practice has contributed to the erroneous belief that the economic realm lies outside of, and is in opposition to, the spheres of law and politics. Such a dubious supposition has consequences – few of them good, and none of them enlightening. Moreover, a rudimentary knowledge of the principles of property and contract law opens our minds to their inherent complexity, contingency, and importance. This knowledge, in turn, illuminates some of the strengths and weaknesses of markets as economic and social institutions.

Lectures II through VI develop several "ideal types" of markets. Lecture II should be the most familiar. Indeed, readers with a background in conventional economics may wish to skip it. The ideal type of market drawn in that lecture is for non-status goods used in everyday consumption, the essential properties of which can be discerned through immediate inspection – what in the pages of this book will be termed "commodities." It will be posited that these commodity markets operate in the manner supposed in conventional introductions to economics. This exposition will be followed by successive lectures on the markets for credit, assets, and labor. In each instance it will be demonstrated that when a critical element of the "real world" is incorporated into the construction of the theory's core assumptions, the analysis must be modified. Readers will find that these modifications affirm what our personal and collective experience have previously demonstrated. In this sense, these lectures are consistent with our understanding of the institutions and practices of our world. This is in contrast to the rhetoric of market fundamentalism, which tends to hide its radical agenda for privatization and deregulation under a shroud of "objective social science."

Each of the presentations of "non-commodity" markets – credit, assets, and labor – will be analysed through a modified "Supply and Demand" framework. I am aware that this depiction can, in itself, be criticized. But such considerations and reservations will not be addressed here. In this book it will be supposed that the "Supply and Demand" framework can be generalized if it is done with care. But full disclosure mandates that readers know that this venerable theory has been subjected to important, if advanced and technical, criticisms. That said, I believe that it retains an important place in expositions of elementary economics. This, ultimately, is the reason that I continue to believe that the best course is to restructure and reposition this theory, rather than to simply discard it.

From their number it is evident that labor markets are at the core of the following lectures (numbers V through VIII). This is appropriate for several reasons. First, most people earn their living by selling their ability and willingness to work. Second, the object exchanged in such a market, labor, can not be alienated from its possessor: its essence is our time, our selves, in an important sense our very lives and persons. Due to labor's importance, and its unique personal and ethical qualities, a clear understanding of this market is central to any coherent reformulation of the elements of economic theory.

Two lectures on discrimination, a specialized subject within the larger theory of labor economics, are included as this issue has substantial political and economic consequence. Additionally, I believe that this inclusion is important as "economic" arguments have held a prominent place in the rhetoric of those opposed to addressing discriminatory practices through legislation. For these reasons clarity on this sensitive subject is essential.

The last lecture makes a relatively simple point, but in light of the hegemony of market fundamentalist thinking it needs restating. With "the market" now dominating so many personal, political, and even ethical discussions, it is ever-more essential to retain and rearticulate the distinction between moral values and market prices. It may be interesting to know that this lecture was originally presented on the final day of the Fall semester of 2001. Its inspiration was the following reflection: in 2001, the starting wage of a New York City firefighter was less than $40,000. Some of the last people to escape the North Tower of the World Trade Center (the second to fall), told interviewers that many of the firefighters still inside the building knew that the other tower had collapsed. Hence they must have known that the tower they were in would, in all probability, soon do the same. What, then, kept these brave persons at their stations? Clearly, it was a sense of duty – the immemorial duty of all firefighters – to rescue people from burning buildings and other disasters. Sadly, the rhetoric of economics, which has a tendency to conflate values and market prices, precludes ideas such as "duty" or "identity." The unfortunate spread of this conflation into discussions of public policy affirms that a restatement of this distinction is essential. It may be the single most important task of these lectures.

In hindsight, it was especially poignant that this reminder of the existence of duties, duties beyond that of performing contracted-for services for remuneration, took place in New York City. Let us recall that this city had just been at the epicenter of a stock market bubble in which legions of professionals who also had an obligation to protect the public – accountants, senior executives of corporations, lawyers, brokers, and analysts – had knowingly, cynically, and with little in the way of social sanction or legal penalty, abandoned their (substantially less dangerous) fiduciary duties. These financial services professionals abandoned their duty, not out of an understandable fear for their own lives, but simply because they saw an opportunity to supplement their already bloated incomes with other people's money. In such a context New Yorkers, along with the rest of the world, were genuinely moved to discover that after two decades of rampant greed and cynicism on the part of so many wealthy, pampered, and over-compensated professionals, a large number of otherwise humble, unknown, and underpaid residents of the city would risk, and lose, their lives to "do the right thing." That day, a number of "regular joes" demonstrated that market prices do not reflect moral values. Inspired by such heroic deeds, this last chapter reexamines the several meanings that can, or should, be ascribed to the term "choice." Specifically, it considers some of the non-economic elements that enter into consumption decisions and some of the implications that follow from them.

To reiterate, the premise of this book is that it would be an error to presume that the lessons derived through a study of one type of market can be transferred, without reflection or modification, to another. As economics students have observed for decades, the "Real World" matters. Context, idiosyncratic uniqueness, and particularities can make a difference. The question is what contexts, what uniqueness, what particularities, are those that are critical? Moreover, how can these be expected to impact the market? If these last questions are important, and I believe that they are, it follows that in selecting or evaluating policies we must be careful to assess what kind of market is being examined, its underlying structure, and how these factors can be expected to modify expected outcomes.

Finally, a brief conclusion reflects on some of the policy implications that plausibly follow from the reformulation of economics presented in these lectures. What are the implications for our understanding of market regulations? What implications follow if we wish to live in a society committed to individual liberty? Specifically, what are the implications for liberty in both its senses, that is to say our "freedom from" arbitrary interference, in addition to the positive "freedom to" strive to achieve our ends in life (Berlin 1969, Ch. 3)? These crucial questions are, clearly, beyond the scope of a brief book on the elements of economic theory. But the several suggestions or implications advanced there may help to illustrate the several points made previously in the text, and underscore their importance for larger questions of economic policy-making. But, above all, even if I fail to convince my readers of the merits of my arguments, I do hope that I may nevertheless succeed in keeping them interested and perhaps even motivated to question the fundamental preconceptions of market fundamentalism. If I succeed in that, writing this book would have been well worth the effort.

NOTES

1. A simple way to trace these trends is to compare earlier and more recent editions of Paul Samuelson's *Principles of Economics*, a text that played an enormous role in economics instruction from the early 1950s to the late 1970s. Indeed, one reason for the decline in the hegemony of Samuelson's text was its identification with the postwar "Keynesian" consensus and hence its inability, despite revisions, to fully identify with the market fundamentalism that became so pronounced in the 1980s.
2. This latter term reflects the long-standing and powerful consensus between the World Bank, the International Monetary Fund, and the United States Treasury on how Third World economies should be managed. A consequence of their collective economic power, especially in public and private credit markets, is that most nations believe that they had little choice but to follow the dictates of these institutions. In this sense, what Americans have learned to call "globalization" is anything but "inevitable." But this is the subject for another essay.

LECTURE I

Property, contract, and the theory of exchange

> The English economists have taken the laws of private property for granted, assuming that they are fixed and immutable in the nature of things, and therefore needed no investigation. But such laws are changeable – they differ for different peoples and places, and they have profound influence upon the production and distribution of wealth.
>
> John Commons (1893 [1963], p. 59)

> Wealth, in a commercial age, is made up largely of promises.
>
> Roscoe Pound (1922 [1982], p. 133)

ECONOMICS AND THE "THEORY OF THE MARKET"

While some changes have been evident over the last several decades, the above observation by John Commons remains largely accurate. Typically, and naively, most economists adhere to Jean Baptiste Say's dictum: "Political Economy recognizes the right of property solely as the most powerful of all encouragements to the multiplication of wealth, and is satisfied with its actual stability, without inquiring about its origins or its safeguards" (Say, as quoted in Ely, 1914, p. 63). To Say and most economists after him, property rights are a fixed and unproblematic set of laws or rules.

This failure is exacerbated by textbook presentations of market relations that take the definition and meaning of a "commodity" to be given and self-evident. This lack of concern for specifics is aggravated when an abstract good, by tradition termed a "widget," is used to illustrate the "essence" of the market process. In this pedagogy, the student's attention is then directed to the theory of exchange and price. It concludes once the student has been successfully drilled in "the theory of the market."

This overly-abstract pedagogy obscures the institutional structures that are the foundation of market economies. One consequence of this way of thinking is the often repeated and largely fatuous dichotomy between government "regulation" and the "free market" that has become a staple of American political discourse. Another regrettable consequence is that in the making of economic policy, the legal foundations of market systems are either overlooked or, even worse, taken for granted. The debacle remembered as the "Russian transition to capitalism" is only one, terribly tragic, manifestation of this now-conventional error (Holmes, 1997).

The following observation might appear to be trivial: if exchange is the fundamental event in a market economy, then this exchange must be of some object, promise, service or privilege. Moreover, as members of a society, it should be self-evident that we are not at liberty to exchange anything at all. Even in a libertarian utopia one must first establish one's ownership of, or legal authority over, any object, promise, service or privilege that one proposes to sell. Furthermore, each party to an exchange must, at a minimum, be judged "competent" to enter into it. Children and those adults legally declared incompetent are examples of persons who may not enter into legally binding contracts.

History teaches us that conventional definitions as to who qualifies as a legitimate owner of property has changed. For example, in most western societies married women were long considered to be ineligible to own or exchange certain forms of property. Women in general were often, and to a lesser extent still are, forbidden to enter into certain kinds of labor contracts. In the United States most convicted felons may not own (and therefore may not exchange) firearms. Children are prohibited from engaging in a wide variety of labor contracts and, in the United States, may not legally purchase, own, or possess tobacco or liquor.

In short, property is neither a simple nor immediate relation between a person and a thing (Appadurai, 1986; Radin, 1996). On the contrary, property is an artifact of a complex set of social relations: "The essence of property is in the relations among men arising out of their relations to things" (Ely, 1914, p. 96). As with all social relations, the conventional rules and laws governing property are subject to important modifications as values, norms, and technologies change. Like the society in which they are embedded, property and contract law are constantly, and necessarily, in flux. Moreover, their specific manifestation has a complex and potentially important impact on the performance of markets, the productivity of the economy, the outcome of exchanges, and the distribution of wealth and income that can be expected to follow from economic activities (North, 1990; Lazonick, 1991).

PROPERTY LAW

What may be owned, and thereby exchanged, is contingent upon the law of property. While complex in practice, property law is simple in its conception. Traditionally, the law recognizes a property relation when an object, promise, service, or privilege is thought to be owned "free and clear." The underlying principle at work, one that dates back to the time of the famous legal scholar William Blackstone, is that a property claim indicates that someone has a "right of exclusive disposal" over the object in question. The importance of this definition, and its long-standing status, is evident in the following quotations by several prominent economists well-versed in the legal foundations of market processes:

> The institution of property, when limited to its essential elements, consists in the recognition, in each person, of a right to exclusive disposal of what he or she have [sic] produced by their own exertions, or received either by gift or fair agreement, without force or fraud, from those who produced it. (Mill, 1904, p. 278)

> For our present purpose we may define private property as the exclusive control over valuable things by private persons. It is to be distinguished from mere possession. The possessor has the use of the thing for the time being, but unless he is at the same time the owner, he is dependent upon the will of another for the use of it. Ownership implies the right of excluding other persons from the enjoyment of a thing. (Ely et al., 1914, p. 20)

> The appropriation found in property is exclusive in its nature, and carries with it as an attribute the right of the proprietor *to control the action of others in respect to the objects of property*. (Ely, 1914, p. 132, emphasis in the original)

If a person's right to exclusive control over his or her property is to be substantial, they must be able to legitimately call upon the support of the state's police powers. This must be the case if property rights are to be founded upon law rather than superior force. This latter point is a core aspect of the definition of property:

> The exclusive right must be recognized and guaranteed effectively by third parties. If I defend my exclusive right of control over some valuable thing against your claim simply by the strength of my right arm, I have not thereby established the right of private property. My exclusive right of control must be recognized by others and must be maintained by them. (Ely et al., 1914, p. 20)

An implication of Richard Ely's statement is that those who enjoy the right of property have implicitly accepted an important social duty: to respect and uphold the property rights of others. Again, while this duty is easy to delineate conceptually, it is more challenging to describe what it means in actual practice – indeed, this difficulty is one of the reasons our society has judges. Nevertheless, without the mutual recognition of property rights, the concept has no operative meaning:

> The sphere of contract is made up of this mediation whereby I hold property not merely by means of a thing and my subjective will, but by means of another person's will as well and so hold it in virtue of my participation in a common will. (Hegel, 1976, p. 57)

The scope of this recognition, and the duties that it implicitly imposes, have presented the courts and the polity with a number of difficult decisions over the years.

For example, as part of my right to exclusive disposal, I may exchange my wristwatch for cash or drive over it with my car. No individual is legally entitled to interfere with either of these actions. Indeed, I can legitimately anticipate and expect the state to act to defend my right to engage in either course of action.

As is well known, this simple notion of property is presented with an important limit when the exercise of my right to "exclusive disposal" interferes with another person's right to the use of their property. For instance, if I were to drive my car into your legally parked car, I would be infringing on your right to "dispose" of your automobile as you see fit.

Indeed, this simple vision of "exclusive disposal" begins to break down when we consider more complex forms of property such as land because, in most cases, it is difficult to isolate one person's land from the surrounding community. It follows that the set of restrictions that circumscribe the rights of an owner are relatively numerous in the case of property in land. For instance, if I decide to host a rock-and-roll concert or locate a toxic waste dump on my property in a suburban neighborhood, I should anticipate legal challenges. This is because virtually every community that we know of has enacted restrictions on the use of land. These have varied widely. They include prohibitions on the use of lawnmowers before the hour of noon on Sunday, the establishment of businesses that feature nude dancing, the sale of alcohol, the discharge of firearms, the posting of garish signs, or the display of "tacky" commercial art. The list of restrictions is close to endless.

Richard Ely (1914) distinguished between the "extensive" and "intensive" rights of property. By an extensive right, Ely was referring to the breadth and variety of objects, promises, services, or privileges that one could claim as one's property. For instance, we know that we currently enjoy the right to possess toys, food, computers, our own labor, etc. That this extensive margin moves over time is evident when we recall that we may no longer own persons, certain endangered species of animals, several varieties of explosives and weapons systems, and a select group of recreational intoxicants.

By "intensive" property rights, Ely refers to the variety of activities for which we may use our property. As mentioned above, we may drive our own cars over our own wristwatches or we may read our own books. However, we may not build on our own wetlands without attending to certain restrictions that were not in existence only a couple of decades ago. History demonstrates that these "intensive" margins of property rights are continually subject to modification and change. An example of evolving intensive property rights includes the many restrictions on the use of tobacco that have recently swept across the United States. Previously one could smoke virtually everywhere. This is no longer the case.

Finally, technical change means that new and unimagined property rights, along with associated restrictions, are constantly emerging. Technologies give rise to new experiences and products over which society must establish property relations and, consequently, claims to state protection. One striking example involves the airspace over the Grand Central Terminal Building in New York City which is leased to the owners of a separate building. Software and "intellectual property" raise a host of new legal issues, many of which lack obvious answers (cf. Lessing, 2001, 2004). A recent, and legally complex, dilemma concerns the use of cell phones that can take photographs which may then be loaded onto the internet. What restrictions can or should be placed on this technology? What "reasonable" expectation of privacy does one have when in public? At the beach or a public pool? In a public changing room at that same pool? All of these questions will be addressed, sooner of later, by legislation, case law, and lawsuits.

Decisions over the extensive and intensive margins of ownership will always and, in the light of changing technological and social conditions, necessarily be the subject of ongoing political debate. This debate will be influenced by the actual qualities of the technologies themselves in addition to the political and economic decisions of large numbers of people. Throughout American history, judge-made or common law has been concerned with expanding, contracting, and adjudicating the domain of property rights in such a manner that, ideally, is consistent with previous decisions while allowing for the modifications of rights and protections to account for changing realities. Good, and lasting, decisions are typically those consistent with the social practices, values, and welfare of the larger society (Cardozo, 1922). But important exceptions to this principle can readily be identified.[1]

It should be no surprise that some people, people with competing interests, will be displeased with some of the decisions that emerge as the laws of property evolve. One reason is that in almost every instance a modification in the law of property results in a redistribution of wealth and opportunity. Even in the event that a decision is in the overall interest of society, some persons will gain at the real or perceived expense of others. Environmental laws are notoriously of this quality. Restrictions that apply to building on wetlands or ban "clear-cuts" on privately-owned woodlots, often reduce the wealth of those firms or individuals who currently own claims on the lands in question.

Consider, as a particularly dramatic example, the decision to emancipate the slaves. Two prominent economic historians have estimated that at the beginning of the Civil War slaves represented 45.8% of the total wealth of all the free residents of the five primary cotton-growing Southern states. Clearly emancipation represented a tremendous loss for Southern slaveholders (Ransom and Sutch, 1977, pp. 52–3). This being the case, it would have been surprising if Southern planters did not vigorously resist the changing definition of property law proposed by ante-bellum abolitionists.[2]

Another area of difficulty concerns the "ownership" of one's own body. Is it inalienable? Can one sell it, that is to say voluntarily enter into a slavery contract? Can it be "rented," as in the case of prostitution? If the answer to this last question is "no," the implication is that we do not have an absolute property claim in our own sexuality (although under current law, one does in several Nevada counties). By contrast to current practice, can individuals make a constitutional claim to the absolute ownership of their own bodies in all jurisdictions and under all circumstances? Finally, if social norms and the consequent rules of property and contract are to change, who is to be assigned the task of formalizing these changes into law? Every society must address such questions.

Some libertarian philosophers, such as Robert Nozick, argue that property rights should be organized so as to allow individuals maximum freedom – defined as their ability to enter into binding contractual relations (Nozick, 1974). One of his most controversial positions is his argument that individuals should be allowed to sell themselves into slavery. Nozick argues that this possibility would necessarily enhance freedom because it provides people with an additional choice. Such an argument presents us with an interesting conundrum: are we more free if we can "choose" to become slaves? If this seems self-contradictory and for that reason absurd, how about self-enslavement for a limited period of time – such as indentured servitude? Technically, such contracts are no longer legal, but was it not revived when we developed a "volunteer" Army? After all, signing a contract with the Army is not like agreeing to work at a restaurant or accepting a contract to teach economics at Middlebury College. You cannot quit the Army if you decide that you no longer like your platoon sergeant or are subjected to sustained enemy fire. To muddle things further, the military's ability to unilaterally extend enlistments through "stop-loss" orders, as the Bush administration did to staff its adventure in Iraq, enhances the problematic qualities of these contracts (Hockstader, 2004).

Nozick's position can be refuted in the event that we advance what is called a "substantivist" understanding of freedom. According to this view rights, as opposed to privileges, are "inalienable." Substantivists would argue that the maintenance of each individual's capability to live a full life, including his or her ability to enter into future contracts, is fundamental to the state's commitment to protect life, liberty, and property (Mill, 1859; Pound, 1909; Nussbaum, 2000). It follows that a person's liberty is absolute, or "inalienable," and for that reason supersedes their decision to sell themselves into slavery.[3] On the other hand, services or privileges can be alienated. For this reason I can enter into a contract to wash the car of my Dean, or extend to my students the privilege of stopping by my office, without compromising my inalienable liberties.[4]

CONTRACT LAW

According to libertarian political theorists, such as Nozick, the State's role should be limited to the protection of life, property, and the orderly maintenance of freely negotiated contracts (Nozick, 1974). While it is clear that the protection of life and property are the foundation of "freedom" – defined in the negative sense of "freedom from" – the issue is more complex when we consider the law of contract. In a society such as ours, where markets are ubiquitous and the notion of private property is widespread, it is evident that our personal development is dependent upon the acquisition and consumption of a certain mix of objects, promises, services, and privileges that we collectively call "property" (Levine, 1988, 1995). Since we obtain property through inheritance, transfer, creating it ourselves, or contract, it follows that the exchanges governed by contract law are at the foundation of our ability to be free in the positive or substantive sense of "freedom to be."

This "freedom to be" enables us to have some control over who and what we are. This is a personal and fundamental element of freedom for each of us. This positive notion of freedom is more complex than the simpler idea of the state defending our liberties from itself and other individuals. This dual sense of freedom, "freedom from" and "freedom to be," is one of the factors that has made the law of contract so complex over the years.

In its simplest definition, contract law governs the conditions under which property may be exchanged. Our everyday experience confirms that most of the contracts that we enter into are implicit – meaning that they are neither negotiated nor written down. At most a receipt will be offered to mark its completion. That said, many of our most important contracts are explicit (rent, insurance, car payments, etc.). In such cases, each side makes a deliberate effort to stipulate and negotiate the terms of a pending exchange. Given the wide range of contingencies and other considerations, these agreements can evolve into highly complex documents. Even the seemingly mundane task of defining a price can be surprisingly complicated (Morgenstern, 1963, ch. 10).

Even in the case of a most explicit and detailed written contract it is inevitably the case that many aspects of an exchange will remain implicit and open to renegotiation and readjustment (Llewellyn, 1931; Macaulay, 1963; MacNeil, 1974, 1978). If a disagreement over implicit understandings or conditions occurs, the law of contract rules by drawing upon precedent and conventional practice. Fortunately, not every disagreement must result in litigation since the value of an ongoing working relationship often acts as an implicit control mechanism (Llewellyn, 1931; Axelrod, 1984; Milgrom et al., 1990).

A variety of interesting dilemmas emerge in the law of contract when we reflect upon the specific circumstances of the labor market. Labor presents unique difficulties because supplying labor-power almost always involves delivering the service in person. Unlike a wristwatch, which we do not retain any rights over after an exchange, the most that we can do with our persons is to "rent" our labor-power. Moreover we, and the state in its role as the guarantor of our rights, retain a compelling interest in our health and welfare while we are on the job. This means that some protections or guarantees must be mandated, negotiated, and/or compensated for. At a minimum, the specific qualities of the work conditions will be of interest to both parties. As Ely put it, "The fact that the function of working is bound up with the rest of a human personality gives the purchaser control over other parts of the worker's life than those which he has directly bought" (Ely, 1914, p. 627).

Since the state is obligated to protect its citizens' "life, liberty, and property," and enforce contracts, labor law can be the object of intense political interest and debate. Over the centuries, labor law has undergone some dramatic changes. Legislation and court decisions concerning maximum hours, health and safety, minimum wages, and the right to unionize have each and severally had a profound impact upon the form and content of American labor relations (Hovenkamp, 1988; Paulsen, 1996; Nordlund, 1997; Steinfeld, 2001; Linder, 2002).

Important and lasting changes in the distribution of wealth, income, and opportunity have followed from these decisions.

THE CONDITIONS FOR A LEGALLY "BINDING" CONTRACT

At its simplest level, a contract is an offer and an acceptance. However, for a contract to be considered legally binding, in the sense of being formally recognized and therefore enforceable by the legal system, the following criteria must be met: (a) no coercion must be exerted or implied, (b) consideration must be paid, and (c) the contract must be consistent with the laws of the land.

(A) No Coercion

The no coercion rule is easy to articulate. In practice, it has led to controversy and extensive debate. In its simplest form this rule affirms our common sense belief that our consent to the armed robber's terms of "your money or your life" does not constitute a binding contract. Any contract entered into under the threat of violence is not legally binding.

While no coercion is an unambiguous rule, how do we assess an implicit threat? What if an "amorous" boss invites his new executive assistant to accompany him on a summer weekend to his beachside house? What if the invitation comes with a suggested, if unspoken, implication that it would be "unwise" to refuse such an invitation? Alternatively, what if a large and physically fit person "asks" you to buy a brick for $40 on a dark lonely street? What if this same person insists that you consider their "offer" while holding the brick in question up in your face? In neither of the above cases has a threat been stated. But is one implied? On what grounds should the courts decide? Does the specific identity and role of each of the individuals, and the setting of the "negotiation," determine the case? Should an *a priori* abstract principle or rule decide the merits of each case? Many of us would agree that context is an important element of justice, but what weight should be assigned to it in matters of law? The complexity of each of the above scenarios is related to the fact that context is difficult to account for in matters of law since "equality of treatment" and "reasonableness" are each highly valued as legal and social ideals (Rose, 1988).

Throughout American economic history the courts have had to address situations wherein economic duress has led people to enter into contracts that they would otherwise reject. People have accepted, and still accept, contracts that amount to a condition of slavery in everything but name as a consequence of their poverty or indebtedness at the time of its negotiation (Ransom and Sutch, 1977, ch. 8; Bales, 1999). Should we conclude that such contracts are "freely" negotiated and entered into? What of a case wherein a contract "agreed to" in the face of poverty forces a person into even more extreme misery in an inevitable and self-reinforcing cycle?

Some legal and political theorists have argued that economic desperation is in itself coercive and thus a form of injustice. Among others, this argument was made a hundred years ago by a group of British political theorists who came to be known as the "New Liberals" (Hobhouse, 1911 [1994]; Green, 1881 [1986]). Here in the United States, the economist Richard Ely termed contracts agreed to under economic duress "the new feudalism" (Ely, 1914, pp. 711–29). Many Progressive and New Deal Era reformers agreed with him. Among them was the prominent Catholic theologian and labor rights activist Monsignor John A. Ryan:

> When a labourer is compelled by dire necessity to accept a wage that is insufficient for a decent livelihood, his consent to the contract is free only in a limited and relative way. It is what the moralists call *"voluntarium imperfectum."* It is vitiated to a substantial extent by the element of fear, by the apprehension of a cruelly evil alternative. The labourer does not agree to this wage because he prefers it to any other, but merely because he prefers it to unemployment, hunger, and starvation. (Ryan, 1919, p. 329)

The concern to check the coercive nature of economic need motivated the demand for laws regulating work hours and minimum wages that began during the early decades of the twentieth century (Prasch, 1998b, 1999, 2000c; Levin-Waldman, 2001, ch. 3). This Progressive-era concern for the injustice that was a predictable consequence of economic coercion later inspired the labor and welfare-state legislation that we now associate with President Franklin Roosevelt's New Deal. But this was not a seamless transition. Economic legislation was treated most skeptically by the courts that, by 1900, had come to favor a doctrine known as "Liberty of Contract."

In an (in)famous United States Supreme Court decision, known as "The Bakers' Case," the majority ruled, five-to-four, that the State of

New York was infringing on bakery employees' constitutionally protected "Liberty of Contract" when it enacted a law limiting their working day to 10 hours (*Lochner* vs. *New York*, 198 U.S. 45 (1905)). The court ruled that the Fourteenth Amendment to the Constitution guaranteed that "life, liberty, and property" could not be taken without "due process of law." This decision was based upon an expansive interpretation the Fourteenth Amendment, an amendment originally passed to protect the rights of recently emancipated slaves. As Justice Oliver Wendell Holmes argued in his dissent to the court's majority, "The Fourteenth Amendment does not enact Mr. Herbert Spencer's *Social Statics* . . . a constitution is not intended to embody a particular economic theory, whether of paternalism and the organic relation of the citizen to the State or of *laissez-faire*" (Holmes, dissent in *Lochner*, op. cit.). Nevertheless, the court's majority held that an absolute liberty of contract was the relevant legal principle in this case. Again, can a freely negotiated contract between a party that is economically desperate, and another that is not, be coercive? After all, the bakery owners were not forcing their employees to accept onerous terms. These employees, according to the majority opinion of the court, were free adult males who had freely contracted with bakery owners. Employers could also, with reason, argue that they were not responsible for the preexisting poverty, difficult circumstances, and reduced bargaining power of their employees. The claim that the State of New York made, but failed to sustain in this case, was that a labor market could be coercive even when the terms of employment are the outcome of a formally free and fair negotiation.

Since the 1930s, legislatures and the courts have generally found that an unequal bargain, with a detrimental result, can occur even in the event of an otherwise freely negotiated labor contract. Furthermore, they have held that the state, in its role as society's guarantor of its citizens' liberties, can proscribe contracts that are deemed, *a priori*, to be detrimental to the health and welfare of individuals and the market system considered as a whole. For this reason protective labor laws, such as the minimum wage, have been upheld (Paulsen, 1996; Nordlund, 1997).

By contrast with the dominant perspective of the American public and the legal profession, over the past 50 years American economists have generally rejected the proposition that systematically unequal exchanges can occur in a free and fair market. Given their prior commitment to models of the market made up of free, autonomous, and rational agents, economists have been critical of much of the labor market legislation passed by legislatures and upheld by the courts since the late 1930s (Stigler, 1946; Friedman, 1962). Much of the dissension between the economics and legal professions is a consequence of these different "visions." This debate has fueled the emergence of a "law and economics" movement committed to reinserting the liberty of contract perspective into legal discourse and, ultimately, judicial rulings (Purdy, 1998).

(B) Consideration

Readers should be warned that the law of consideration is a very complicated subject, and for this reason what follows here should be thought of as suggestive rather than definitive. With this caveat in mind, at its most general level consideration is "the price paid for the promise" (American Institute of Banking, 1940, p. 48). Often it is the full amount owed, but it could be a down payment, a symbolic sum, or even a gesture. Today, the latter is generally a signature, performed to indicate the acceptance of the terms, and thereby the intention to be bound by the terms of the contract. Historically, the terms of consideration were thought to be fulfilled when one party bestowed a benefit upon the contract's counter-party, thereby demonstrating that one had incurred a detriment in exchange for the contract. Again, the consideration offered need not represent the full value of the benefits promised under the contract and may even consist of a token such as a single dollar. Today clear intent, as represented by a formal seal or signature, is typically sufficient to indicate acceptance. Under either approach, consideration is a gesture that signals that you have knowingly, and with intent, bound yourself to fulfill the terms of the contract.

Consideration also serves to distinguish a "contract" from a "gift." Since the days of ancient Rome, contract law has tried to distance itself from the task of ensuring that people keep promises to bestow gifts upon one another (as always, exceptions can be found). A contract is legally distinguished from a gift in that the latter is thought to be what lawyers call a gratuitous undertaking. By contrast, a contract is an exchange negotiated between, and involving the agency of, separate and responsible parties. A gift, by contrast to a contract, is not thought to involve intent, payment, or performance on the part of those upon whom it is bestowed.

(C) Consistent with the Laws of the Land

Private contractual relationships cannot preempt the state's laws. For example, one cannot be released from prison or excused from the military draft by contracting to work at the local country club. Additionally, if fulfilling the terms of a contract necessitates a violation of the law, then it will neither be recognized nor upheld by the courts. The purpose of this latter provision is to disrupt the formation of orderly markets in illegal products or services. Absent any recourse to the courts for adjudication of disputes, contract enforcement in such markets can be expected to be inefficient, expensive, and even dangerous. In short, the absence of legally enforceable contracts and property rights collectively increase the costs associated with operating an illicit business. As a consequence the total volume of illegal business should decrease. Depending upon circumstances, the total revenues that accrue to such businesses may or may not decrease. The latter outcome depends upon several considerations that are beyond the concerns of this lecture.

As an adaptive response to the lack of enforceable contracts, illegal markets are often characterized by an emphasis on reputation. This element of illegal markets has been popularized in books and films on the Italian Mafia, which seem to marvel at these "Codes of Honor." Economically speaking having a reputation for integrity, and the "respect" of everyone in a market, are substantial competitive advantages in the absence of legally enforceable contracts. A credible reputation reduces both bargaining and enforcement costs. Additionally, since one cannot sue for breach of contract in these markets, violence is periodically visited upon those who are thought to be in violation of the terms of their obligations (Bourgois, 1995). The other side of this story is that persons who wish to break their agreements must do more than simply appear in bankruptcy court. They might be better advised to leave town so as to avoid the draconian penalties periodically exacted for non-compliance.

CONCLUSION

As is evident from the above, the social institution that we term "the market" is a complex construction, based on an evolving system of rights, property law, and contract law. While often overlooked, one could plausibly argue that economic progress is as much the consequence of advances in the formation of the social institutions that support the division of labor and exchange, including the law of property and contract, as it is a consequence of technology or the sum of individual or collective enterprising activities (Commons, 1924; Chandler, 1977; North, 1990; Lazonick, 1991; Steinfeld, 2001). In this sense, the study of market relations properly begins with an understanding of these laws and institutions. It follows that economic policy and economic change should be at least as concerned with "getting institutions right," or "getting the legal framework right."

An analysis of economic affairs necessarily begins with a study of economic institutions – the most important being the foundational structures of the market itself – property and contract law. It is also evident that the social scientific and policy question is not whether the law or the state is involved in the market. Rather the correct question is just how it should be involved, and what laws and regulations make the most sense. In short, "regulation" is not necessarily in conflict with "the market." On the contrary, the social arrangement that is conventionally called a "free market" has been built upon a long and evolving tradition of legally framed rights, distinctions, and prohibitions that is continually interacting with an equally long history of evolving ideas, legislation, and court rulings on property and contract law.

NOTES

1. An interesting instance of these considerations taking place as I write is the effort to convince Americans and the world that the use of file-sharing software to transfer music or movies is "theft," even "piracy"! In this instance, technology has created new possibilities for human behavior and action. For obvious reasons, the film and movie industries desire to control this process and have used their considerable influence to achieve this result. Rhetorically, they have brought the language of "theft," against which there is a strong and lasting association with immorality, to an issue which is really one in which new technologies have created a legal vacuum. As a legal and social issue, this ongoing process is similar to that of the colonial era in the United States when the new settlers found that they had easy access to large stands of old-growth timber, including many trees with long, straight trunks. The English crown claimed prior ownership of all such trees as they were valuable for the masts of ships. The colonists valued them for building homes and fences. Since the felling of trees on what settlers took to be "unclaimed" land was something that colonists could readily do, and since the Crown had a limited ability to enforce its claim, it is not surprising that many colonists harvested these tall straight trees for their own use.

2. Adam Smith thought that such considerations were paramount even in relatively pious societies: "The late resolution of the Quakers in Pennsylvania to set at liberty all their negro slaves, may satisfy us that their number cannot be very great" (Smith, 1776 [1937], p. 366).
3. In Germany a person entered into a fully voluntary agreement to be killed and cannibalized. Later his killer presented overwhelming proof to the court that this individual's death was part of voluntary contract. The court nevertheless set aside these agreements and found the defendant guilty of manslaughter (Landler, 2004).
4. Not everyone would agree with this sentence. Several economists have argued that the labor contract is inherently a violation of a worker's freedom, and that the nation's workplaces should be reorganized as worker-owned cooperatives to eliminate the need for them (Ellerman, 1990, 1992; Lutz, 1999).

LECTURE II

Commodity markets: the economics of a "spot" contract

It needs to be stated at the outset that Supply and Demand is, at best, a tendency and not a "Law." Unfortunately, the rhetoric indulged in by too many economists, paid consultants, opinion page writers, and other sundry "experts" has so undermined our thinking that this must be clearly stated. With this preliminary out of the way, we can state that our collective experience with markets suggests recurrent tendencies or trends. Upon considering these tendencies, economists and others have perceived persistent patterns. As a consequence, early social scientists developed a set of metaphysical propositions concerning the "innate" nature of people and, by extension, market processes.[1] These metaphysical notions include propositions such as "people are rational" and "people are self-interested." From these ideas it is deduced that people will invariably search out the best products at the lowest prices, all other things being equal.[2] As discussed in the introduction, I am partial to such views. However I also believe that an accurate understanding of how markets work requires *Theories*, rather than a single *Theory*, of Supply and Demand.

The market to be examined in this lecture will be labeled the "commodity market." I need to emphasize, here at the beginning, that in these lectures the word "commodity" has a specific definition. In these lectures, commodities are commonplace or everyday items used for personal consumption.[3] It will be assumed that the use or display of these items confers neither status nor superior reputation on those owning, using, or displaying them.[4] It follows that the exclusive reason that a consumer buys a commodity is to satisfy a well-defined want or need. Examples of commodities, in the sense I am using the term here, would include dishwashing soap, broccoli, or athletic socks.

Another critical quality of commodities, as they will be presented
here, is that they are "inspection goods." These are best defined in
contrast to "experience goods" – whose underlying or innate qualities only come to be revealed after purchase and use. Contrary to
experience goods, the relevant qualities of inspection goods can be
readily ascertained by relatively uninformed buyers through direct
observation.

Two important presuppositions are consistent with the above
considerations. First, consumers can be presumed to have reasonably
complete knowledge of the qualities of the several commodities competing in any given market. Second, aside from the influence of broad
cultural norms, consumers' demand for commodities are substantially formed independently of one another. The implication is that
each consumer's choices and sets of final demands are established
independently of the assessment of other consumers in the market or
society.[5]

THE THEORY OF DEMAND FOR COMMODITIES

Demand is represented as a schedule depicting the quantities of a
good that people are willing to buy per unit of time, at varying prices,
all other things being held constant. When the price of a commodity
is reduced, people will exhibit a higher quantity demanded of a commodity. Again, all other things being equal. Similarly, the higher the
price, the less quantity demanded *ceteris paribus* (Translated, this
means the condition of "all other things being equal").[6]

In Figure II.1, demand is presented as a schedule where the quantity demanded (D) is inversely related to price (P). Starting on the left,
we can see that when the price is relatively high (P_a), the associated
level of demand is low (Q_a). As this price declines toward zero, the
quantity demanded (Q) increases. This tendency is illustrated by the
slope of the demand schedule (D), in which ever-lower prices (P) are
shown as corresponding to ever-higher quantities being demanded
(Q). (Read the above diagram like a book – from left to right.)

It should be noted here that the convention for graphical formats
is that price movements induce changes in the *quantity demanded*, and
are depicted by movements along a fixed demand schedule. This is
illustrated in Figure II.2 below by the movement from point A to

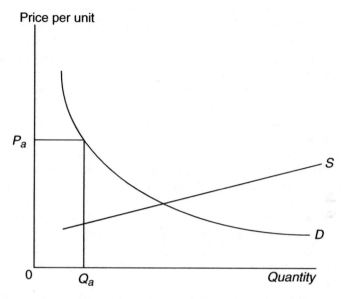

Figure II.1 Supply and demand of a commodity

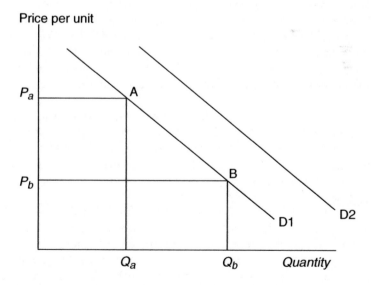

Figure II.2 Shift in demand (D1 to D2) vs. change in the quantity demanded (A to B)

point B. By contrast, what is termed an increase in *demand* is graphically signified by shifting the entire schedule to the right. This is illustrated in Figure II.2 by a shift in the entire demand schedule from D1
to D2. To review, then, price changes induce changes in the *quantity
demanded* and are illustrated by movements along a fixed demand
schedule. Changes in the level of demand *from any cause other than
the price of the commodity* are illustrated by shifting the entire schedule either outward to the right (for increases) or inward to the left (for
decreases).

The core principle underlying the theory of demand is the idea of
"substitution." Customers are thought to be, explicitly or implicitly,
comparing and contrasting the price and qualities of this and other
commodities with the size of their budget and the intensity of the
wants or needs they are hoping to satisfy. Should it turn out that,
after all relevant prices are considered, a rival good with similar qualities would more completely satisfy the consumer's wants, or satisfy
them more cheaply, then the customer will purchase in that other
market.

It is this all-important principle, called "The Substitution Effect,"
that accounts for the slope of the demand curve. The slope of the line,
moving downward to the right, graphically illustrates the idea of an
inverse relationship between price and the quantity demanded – when
one rises, the other falls, and vice versa. The substitution effect is the
fundamental explanation for why quantity demanded declines as the
price of a commodity increases. When the market price rises, consumers less committed to this specific item will seek out cheaper
substitutes.

In this sense, high prices "ration" goods across all those who might
desire to have it. Markets, of course, do not ration by edict. Rather,
rationing occurs in accordance with both the *willingness* and, equally
importantly, the *ability*, to pay. This fact explains why this mode of
rationing – ability to pay in the market – is favored by people whose
incomes are plentiful relative to their leisure time – that is to say
people with high incomes or substantial wealth. Stated simply, in a
market economy, desire, in the absence of cash, is exclusively a hope,
a wish, or a prayer. Adam Smith summarized the situation long ago,
"A very poor man may be said in some sense to have a demand for a
coach and six; he might like to have it; but his demand is not an
effectual demand, as the commodity can never be brought to market
in order to satisfy it" (Smith 1776 [1937], p. 63).

As mentioned, changes in conditions other than market price are represented by a shift in the overall demand schedule. When these conditions change the entire schedule will shift either inward to the left (meaning lower overall demand at each and every price) or outward to the right (meaning a higher overall demand at each and every price). Conditions that induce such a shift include changes in:

1. The number and average income of current and potential buyers;
2. Buyers' tastes and preferences;
3. The availability or price of goods that are either substitutes or complements to this commodity;
4. The availability and price of consumer credit;
5. The state of consumers' collective expectations as to future market conditions, including the future price and availability of this commodity.

Changes in any of these conditions are thought to induce a shift in the demand schedule. The distance and form of this shift depends upon (a) the size of the changing condition and (b) the responsiveness of consumers to the change in question.

Consumer income plays a crucial role in the demand for commodities. *Ceteris paribus*, higher incomes increase the demand for what are called "normal goods." When incomes rise, people desire more normal goods such as comfortable housing, new automobiles, and Caribbean vacations. People with low or falling incomes reduce their demand for such items (similar dynamics apply to changes in wealth). When incomes rise, the increase in demand is depicted as a shift from D1 to D2 in Figure II.2 above. From this description it is evident that a meal at one of the best restaurants in town can plausibly be thought to be a "normal good." If the community's income rises, we can expect such restaurants to gain additional business, *ceteris paribus*.

The opposite dynamic applies to "inferior goods." Inferior goods are items that we tend to consume less of when our incomes increase. Examples include macaroni and cheese in a box, discount brands of beer, rusted and damaged old cars, etc. If the commodity depicted in Figure II.2 were an inferior good, an increase in income (or wealth) would have the effect of shifting demand downward. In Figure II.2 this would be represented by a shift from D2 to D1.

Not surprisingly, an increase in consumers' "tastes and preferences" in favor of this product shifts the demand curve from D1 to

D2. If an item that is consumed as a complement to this item is cheaper, the quantity demanded of that other good will increase, and the demand curve for the good we are analysing in Figure II.1 will be shifted out to the right. The price of substitutes and the demand for the above good, not surprisingly, are positively correlated. If the price of a close substitute rises, the demand for the above good shifts out, and vice versa. More and cheaper credit operates in a manner parallel to an increase in income and increases the demand for all normal goods.

A final, and important influence on consumer demand comes through expectations. If consumers expect the price of home heating oil to increase in the near future, they will be inclined to refill their home storage tanks today. The result will be an outward shift in this commodity's demand schedule with an increase in the price of oil. This is a direct consequence of the outward shift in the demand schedule, which was itself a consequence of the previously-posited expectation of a rise in price. It should be noted that economic events driven by expectations can take the form of "self-fulfilling prophesies." We will return to this important issue in the lecture on asset markets.

DEMAND ELASTICITY

Understanding the broad causal relationships between price and demand is often inadequate for business and public policy discussions. In addition to "Which way?" one often requires an answer, or at least a defensible guess, as to "How much?" In the event that a firm were to reduce the price of its goods, by how much can they expect the quantity demanded to rise? This issue is addressed by a concept called "elasticity."

The conventional formula for elasticity, given below, is relatively simple. The elasticity of demand (E_d) is *the absolute value* of the percentage change in the quantity demanded $(\%\Delta Q_d)$ induced by a 1 percent change in price $(\%\Delta P)$. If, for convenience, we leave out the signs for absolute value, the formula is as follows:

$$E_d = \%\Delta Q_d / \% \Delta P$$

"Elasticity" is the standard measure of the responsiveness of quantity demanded to changes in price. In plain English, "elasticity" is the absolute value of the percentage change of the quantity demanded induced by a 1 percent change in price. Some numerical examples will illustrate the point. If a 1 percent price reduction were to increase the quantity demanded of an item by 2 percent, we would say that the elasticity of demand for this commodity at this price is 2 and that its demand is "price-elastic" or, more simply, "elastic." Similarly, if a 1 percent decrease in another commodity's price were to induce one-quarter of a percent increase in its quantity demanded, we would say that this item's elasticity is one-quarter and that it is "price-inelastic" or, more simply, "inelastic."

A high elasticity (by convention, an estimated elasticity greater than 1) implies that the quantity demanded of a particular commodity is highly responsive to changes in price. This high level of responsiveness suggests that consumers think of this commodity as either inessential, in that they can get along without it, or that it has a substantial number of close substitutes. For either of these reasons a 1 percent increase in the price of this commodity will result in a greater than 1 percent decrease in the quantity demanded as consumers either stop buying the item altogether or seek out a close substitute. Additionally, a commodity may register a relatively high degree of elasticity when it absorbs a significant portion of the income of its median consumer. The explanation for the latter tendency is that consumers will gather more information and seek out more substitutes when they are spending a large portion of their income.

By contrast, a low elasticity of demand (by convention, a measured elasticity less than 1), can occur when consumers believe that they need this commodity and that its unique attributes render it difficult to identify worthy substitutes over the short or medium period. Such a commodity might even be said to represent a "need" as opposed to a "want." An extreme example would be the demand for insulin on the part of a person living with diabetes.

A low elasticity of demand can also occur when the commodity in question absorbs a trivial percentage of the income of the median consumer. Consumers are less likely to comparison shop if they are spending a minuscule portion of their income on a particular purchase. In the United States today, bulk table salt has this quality. Most of us buy a large container of salt every year or so at prices that, to most Americans, are inconsequential. Since our pattern of salt use is determined by the intersection of lifestyle and cooking habits, and the out-of-pocket cost is trivial, we pay little attention to changes in the price of table salt. As a consequence of our lack of concern the demand for salt is relatively inelastic. Our collective disinterest grants the firms that produce and distribute it more discretion when setting prices.

By contrast to the above example, for most of history salt was inelastic, not because of its low cost relative to people's incomes, but rather because it is necessary to sustain life. Additionally, for a long time it was one of the few available food preservatives. For each of these reasons, salt was often subject to tax, especially on the part of despotic governments – the Emperors of China and the British Raj in India come immediately to mind. It is not a coincidence that when Mahatma Gandhi began his campaign of non-violent resistance against the British Raj one of his first, and most symbolically effective moves, was to march with his colleagues from his Ahmedabad home to the Indian Ocean to produce his own salt. The British, of course, had made it illegal to gather salt directly from the ocean as it was an effective strategy for avoiding their salt tax.

To illustrate the concept of elasticity, consider the effect of a successful advertising campaign. Ostensibly, the purpose of advertising is to notify or remind people of the existence, availability, or price of certain products. Yet it is also evident that advertising is charged with two other important tasks (Bernays, 1928 [2004]; Dawson, 2005). The first is to modify the underlying tastes of the target population in a manner favorable to the supplier of the good or goods in question. This provides a larger number of buyers and for that reason an increase in demand. Second, a successful advertising campaign should convince at least a portion of the buying public that the item in question is a necessity – that is to say, convince the public that few good substitutes exist. Ideally, customers will come to perceive the commodity in question as a "need," rather than as a mere "want." When an advertising campaign achieves such a result, the demand curve becomes steeper.

A highly successful advertising campaign has the collective effect, illustrated in Figure II.3, of shifting the demand schedule outward from D1 to D2 even as, visually, it becomes "steeper." In the shorthand language of economics, it is said that the demand schedule has become more "inelastic." From the perspective of the advertising firm a most cheerful (and remunerative) consequence is that this steeper demand schedule will enable its client to raise the price of its wares without losing too many of its customers – thereby increasing revenues (total revenues are simply price times quantity).

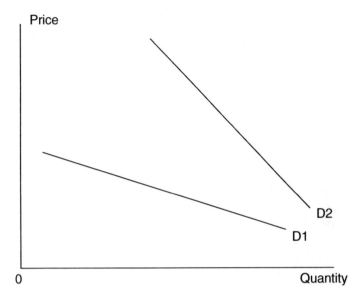

Figure II.3   The effects of successful advertising on demand

THE THEORY OF THE SUPPLY OF COMMODITIES

The supply schedule illustrates a set of prices and the hypothetical quantity of commodities that firms would supply at each of them. In drawing this schedule, it is conventionally supposed that the supply of commodities is limited by at least one fixed factor of production (ie. the factory has a certain capacity, or the farmers' fields are only so large, etc.). This "stylized fact" implies that supply is not unlimited and that some kind of "bottleneck" will emerge as the production of that commodity increases. From this assumption, it is argued that costs-per-unit will tend to rise with increases in the total quantity supplied. In the market for commodities, the price of a commodity and the quantity supplied are thought to be positively related. This means that when the market price rises, the quantity supplied to the market also rises. Graphically, the supply schedule slopes upward to the right, reflecting the increasing costs and, for that reason, increased price that consumers must pay to induce firms to expand supply.[7] Assuming, for simplicity, a linear relationship

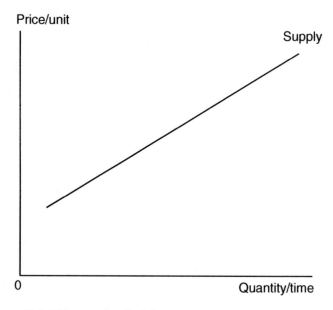

Figure II.4   The supply schedule

between price and quantity supplied, the market supply curve is depicted in Figure II.4.

An important theorem associated with the idea of "perfectly competitive" markets is that at each and every point on the supply schedule prices reflect the additional cost to producers of supplying one more unit of the commodity in question. The cost of this last unit supplied is known as the "marginal cost." This concept is important because, as mentioned, it represents the cost to the firm of producing one additional unit of a commodity. Likewise, it illustrates how much the firm would save if it did not produce that item. In the event that the market price is equal to marginal cost of production, the producer is charging its last consumer a price exactly equal to the direct expense associated with providing that last item. The theorem that at any given moment the supply price is equal to the firm's marginal cost of production is, it cannot be overemphasized, an important conclusion from the perspective of political economy.[8] On the margin, customers get exactly what they pay for, and suppliers are exactly compensated for their direct costs. On the production and sale of this last, or marginal, unit of output neither party to the transaction can be thought to experience either an excess gain or loss.

The core proposition of the previous paragraph is typically demonstrated through a "counter-factual" argument. Consider a firm operating in an environment featuring no costs associated with entering or exiting a market, no costs to making transactions or gathering information, and many competitors – what economists call a "perfectly competitive" market. Now let us suppose that this firm charges its customers a price greater than its marginal cost of production. In such an instance a competing firm, perceiving an opportunity, will be able to enter this market and supply the good for less than the firm of our example. The original firm or even a third firm would then perceive an opportunity to present the item for even less, and so on, until the competitive process forces the market price down to the point where the item is sold at its marginal cost.

A parallel example illustrates what would occur in the event that the market price were lower than the marginal cost of supplying it. Experiencing a loss, firms would, again at no cost, withdraw such items from the market and redeploy their productive assets to more lucrative activities. Customers will then be forced to either pay a higher price for these items or attempt to meet their wants through the purchase of a substitute. The resulting combination of reduced supply by firms, and enhanced price offers by consumers, will induce the market price to rise enough to cover the marginal cost associated with the last unit supplied.

As mentioned, the quantity supplied of a commodity is positively related to its market price. If the market price rises, so will the quantity supplied. If the market price falls, so will the quantity supplied. Besides changes in the market price, which cause movements along a fixed supply schedule, the entire supply schedule will shift as a consequence of changes in the market environment. These conditions fall under one of the following headings:

1. Changes in technology;
2. Changes in the unit cost of inputs into the production process;
3. Changing prices in related markets that firms could readily supply;
4. Changes in the availability and price of business credit;
5. Changing expectations of future market prices and available supplies.

These environmental changes, and their effects, will be addressed in order.

1.   *Changes in technology*   Technology, as used here, is to be understood in a broad sense – that is to say it is more than simply improved "know how" or "machines." It includes new and innovative management styles, techniques for reformulating or reconfiguring the production process, etc. The "stylized fact" I wish to capture here is that technology has the effect of enabling greater production with a fixed number of inputs or the same level of production with a reduced quantity of inputs.[9]

When technology improves, the marginal cost of production for each and every unit is reduced. As a consequence, the entire supply schedule shifts outward and to the right (again, these graphs are read, as books are, from left to right). This shift illustrates that producers are able and willing to supply a greater quantity of goods at each and every market price, *ceteris paribus*. This is illustrated in Figure II.5 below with the shift of the schedule from S_1 to S_2.

Figure II.5   Changes in supply

2. *Changes in the unit cost of production inputs*   Suppose the cost of a critical input were to decrease, reducing the cost of production at each and every level of output. In this case, the entire supply schedule would shift outward and to the right. This illustrates a lower marginal cost of production for each and every unit produced and therefore an increased level of supply at each and every market price. This is consistent with the shift illustrated in Figure II.5. Similarly, in the event of a higher cost of inputs, the marginal cost of production would increase. The supply schedule would be represented as shifting inward and to the left, illustrating a reduced supply at each and every market price, *ceteris paribus*.

High volatility has been a long-standing characteristic of many primary goods that are essential production inputs. Oil, wheat, copper, cocoa, bulk coffee and many other primary goods and natural resources have long exhibited dramatic price fluctuations.[10] These fluctuations, in turn, contribute some risk to the economic system as these price changes impact the cost structure of producing firms, including the average and marginal cost of supplying additional units of output.

3. *Price changes in related markets that firms could supply*   The "stylized fact" here is that the resources and talents at the disposal of any given firm can be redeployed to related markets. Consequently, profit-seeking firms can be expected to monitor prices in related markets to see if potential opportunities emerge. Should a non-trivial number of firms identify a more profitable opportunity in a related market, the supply schedule will shift inward and to the left, which is consistent with a decline in the amount of goods for sale at each and every market price. An example would be the effects of increasing suburban housing prices on the market for locally-grown farm produce. Suburban farmland becomes relatively scarce as it is turned into housing, thereby reducing the supply, while increasing the price, of fresh produce.

4. *Changes in the availability and price of credit*   Firms generally require credit to operate and expand their businesses. Bank credit is important, but of equal if not greater importance is credit from suppliers. Products, machinery, spare parts and even labor are delivered to firms in the expectation that bills (and wages) will be paid at a later date. The period between receiving the items in question and the date that payment is due represents credit to a firm. Unsurprisingly firms

at risk of bankruptcy have difficulty convincing suppliers to deliver goods without advance payment. This increases the cost of doing business as such firms must have substantial cash available "up front" to replenish inventories, buy parts, pay labor, etc.

In the previous paragraph it was mentioned that labor, like other production inputs, is usually supplied on credit. This is largely unrecognized since it is rarely acknowledged and interest is even more rarely paid. Typically, a new employee will work for an extended period, often four to six weeks, before receiving their initial paycheck. Accrued vacations and other benefits, such as a retirement plans, represent additional forms of deferred compensation. Not surprisingly, for many firms, labor is their most substantial creditor. Over the last decades we have been reminded of this fact on almost a daily basis as firms with substantial outstanding debts to their employees, such as airlines or steel companies, have asked the courts to relieve them of these contracted obligations. Be that as it may, the supply curve shifts inward or to the left when less credit is available or more expensive. It shifts outward and to the right when more credit is available or cheaper.

5. *Changing Expectations*   Firms form expectations as to how the markets for inputs and finished goods will look in the near and distant future. If a firm anticipates that the market for a given product is likely to be depressed, they will move now to reduce their inventory of that item. This can be accomplished by placing a greater quantity on the market today. As in the case of demand, there can be an element of a "self-fulfilling prophesy" to this. More supply today means a lower price. Hence, the expectation of a lower price tomorrow can induce firms to take actions today (such as dumping extra inventory) that induces just such a consequence. These dynamics work in the opposite direction in the event that firms anticipate rising prices.

DYNAMICS OF THE "SPOT MARKET" FOR COMMODITIES

First, a definition: a "spot market" is one in which transactions are negotiated and settled in the course of a single meeting or interaction. The paradigmatic example is the neighborhood garage sale.

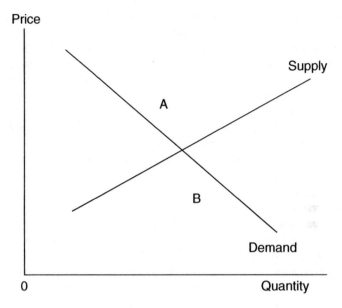

Figure II.6   The spot market for a commodity

Spot markets feature dynamics distinct from markets in which firms or persons enter into "ongoing relationships." Instances of the latter include debt, insurance, or mortgage contracts. The importance of this distinction will emerge in the lecture on credit markets. Commodity markets, the subject of this lecture, will be assumed to be spot markets. With this in mind, consider the graph in Figure II.6, and in particular two points on this graph: Identified by the letters A and B.

In Figure II.6 it is evident that the point marked by the letter A is above the *market equilibrium* consistent with the *market-clearing* price – defined as the unique point where the supply schedule intersects the demand schedule. Since point A is above this equilibrium, and because this graph is read from left to right, it is evident that at point *A* the quantity supplied of this particular commodity is greater than the quantity demanded. Indeed, in the region of the graph around point A, the market is characterized by an excess of supply ($S > D$), otherwise known as a surplus. Given the desire of all profit-oriented firms to sell their wares, the expectation is that they will be inclined to reduce their excess inventory by lowering their prices.

Lower prices will simultaneously increase the quantity demanded. These adjustments will continue until the market clearing price and quantity are established where the quantity demanded and the quantity supplied are equivalent. This is represented by the intersection of these schedules in Figure II.6, which is considered to be the point of "market equilibrium." The point marked B is subject to a similar analysis, with the problem being that this region of the graph features a shortage in which market forces will increase the price until the market clearing equilibrium is achieved.

Market equilibrium is the unique point where the two schedules cross and therefore the quantity supplied is exactly equivalent to the quantity demanded. At this point the market is thought to be in a state of rest – hence the term "market equilibrium." This spot market equilibrium has two properties of great analytical and metaphysical importance. In the absence of any other disturbing cause the equilibrium is both unique and stable. It is *stable* because once it is achieved there is no compelling reason for sellers or buyers to deviate from it. Whoever attempts to do so will experience a loss relative to what they would achieve by operating at the market price and quantity. It is *unique* because the slope of each schedule has a different sign, one positive and the other negative, and for this reason there can, logically, be only a single point of intersection.

Collectively, these two qualities (stability and uniqueness) are important, perhaps the most important, lessons of the Theory of Supply and Demand in commodity markets. In light of their importance, we should pause momentarily and reflect on their implications for political economy.

The theory of the market sketched above supports the prominent political idea that government should have a limited role in the marketplace. The reason is that the theory indicates that freely operating markets will automatically and autonomously establish a set of prices that will coordinate (a crucial word) the decisions of all actual and potential market participants such that all their decisions will be consistent with one another. Government's role would be reduced to attending to the definition and protection of property rights and the enforcement of contracts.

Such a statement is fairly sweeping, but to be fair it does not claim that everyone is delighted with the outcome. Some people may have wished, perhaps even needed, to have been supplied with this commodity at lower prices and, in light of the actually existing equilibrium price, now find that they cannot purchase enough of this good. But, whatever the plight of some individuals, the theory does suggest that the market is "efficient" in the sense that, given the assumptions, customers are receiving the greatest quantity of supply at the lowest possible price. This conclusion can be derived from the previously summarized assumptions and the proposition that the market price is equal to the marginal cost in equilibrium. This is the basis of the conventional claim that the free market is "efficient" and that any deviation from market prices, even deviations that may be valid for political or humanitarian reasons, are *ipso facto* inefficient. This is a powerful normative claim, one with tremendous importance for the many economists who insist that *laissez faire* market policies should be given the broadest possible application.

NEGATIVE FEEDBACK EFFECTS AND THE THEORY OF MARKET EQUILIBRIUM

The above analysis of the spot market for commodities illustrates another important aspect of the theory of commodity markets and the lessons for economic and social policy that can be drawn from it. But first, a short digression into the language of engineering will be necessary.

When engineers speak of adjustment mechanisms, they distinguish between negative and positive feedback systems. This distinction is crucial for mechanism design and performance. One should note at the outset, and this is important, that these classifications *are neither normative nor evaluative*. Rather they are technical. A negative feedback system is one that features automatic built-in equilibrating mechanisms. As a consequence, when such a system is disturbed from a state of rest, one or more counter forces are automatically activated that guide the system back to its initial equilibrium position. The level of water in a bathtub illustrates such dynamics. When the surface is disturbed, gravity will act to return the water level to its prior state of tranquillity. Another example is the household thermostat. By design, this mechanism regulates the heat inside of a home so as to maintain the temperature within a preestablished target range. Should the house become too warm, the thermostat directs the furnace to shut off, thereby cooling the environment. Should the house become too cold, the thermostat directs the furnace to run until the environment is warm again. When functioning properly, the internal temperature of the house fluctuates within a comfortable range.

In commodity markets, negative feedback is thought to operate in an analogous manner. No matter what the initial price, the commodity market is thought to be self-correcting in the sense that market forces induce, independently of any government directive, suppliers and buyers to make decisions that collectively contribute to reestablishing and thereby sustaining the "market equilibrium." If the price is too high, surplus inventory will build up and firms will trim prices. If the initial price is too low, inventories will fall and customers will evince a willingness to pay higher prices thereby inducing firms to raise prices and the quantity supplied.

Commodity markets, thanks to these negative feedback mechanisms, are depicted as being able to achieve a "state of rest" or market equilibrium that is both unique and sustainable in the absence of any new disturbance. That commodity markets are believed to have such a strong self-equilibrating mechanism, one that requires a minimum of information and overt coordination among and between its many individual actors, is a crucial element of the argument for allowing markets to distribute goods (Hayek, 1945; Friedman, 1962).

To further instantiate the role and importance of negative feedbacks in commodity markets, let us briefly consider the opposite proposition. This is a system (or market) that exhibits "positive feedback." In a positive feedback system disturbances are thought to be self-reinforcing and for that reason self-sustaining. When such a system is disturbed from its initial equilibrium point, it continues to move ever further away in a process that is self-reinforcing. In the absence of any outside force that can reestablish and reinforce the initial equilibrium, the inevitable consequence of a disturbance to a positive feedback system is a cumulative process.

In the presence of a positive feedback mechanism, almost any disturbance of the system will continue until a structural transformation occurs. In social, natural, and engineering settings, this almost invariably means that we can expect some sort of disaster. Returning to the above analogy of the thermostat, in the event of a positive feedback mechanism, a house that is too warm would become increasingly hotter, and a chilly house would become increasingly cold. In either case, such a positive feedback mechanism would cause significant damage to the house, damage that would become irreversible if it continued long enough (i.e. a house fire or frozen pipes would result).

For an example of a positive feedback operating in nature, consider an avalanche. The snowfield begins in a state of rest, a condition analogous to the market equilibrium described above. A disturbance, say a traversing moose, creates a disturbance. Under the correct snow conditions, such a small initial disturbance can become self-reinforcing and self-sustaining. The initial disturbance of the snow dislodges more snow, which dislodges even more snow, etc., with the effect of creating an ever-greater movement that spreads to the entire snowfield. Once the snow begins to move it is evident that a return to "equilibrium" – the snowfield in its original state of rest – is unachievable. The cumulative effect is an avalanche which is a disaster for any people, buildings, or villages in the valley. Either way, the result is the structural transformation of the ecology and economy of the valley. To review, the lesson is that positive feedback systems, once in motion, move ever-further away from their initial point of stability.

These several presumptive qualities of commodity markets, as described above, have had a long and distinguished history. Of most importance, they suggest that a free market system can be both decentralized and sustainable. The political implications of positing the existence of a free market featuring an effective negative feedback are worthy of contemplation. In the presence of negative feedback between the current price and the posited equilibrium price, self-interest can be relied upon to generate actions that will collectively cause the market's price to achieve and maintain a stable equilibrium. Self-interested suppliers and buyers can be supposed to make a multitude of independent decisions that collectively have the effect of bringing into existence this unique equilibrium with a minimum of insight, reflection, information, or coordination on the part of any authority or the state.[11] In this sense the market is an instrument, one that "signals" complex conditions and incentives to economic actors. These actors, in turn, do not need to understand the details of market conditions or theories, but only aspire to achieve their own ends through buying or selling profitably. Since markets are thought to convey knowledge of prices and quantities at little cost, they are deemed socially "efficient."

Commodity markets are the "ideal type" of market that has been taught to generations of elementary economics students (again, by commodities, I mean consumer-oriented "inspection goods" that confer neither status nor future wealth on their purchasers). This theory has not performed too badly in performing its core task – to explain short-term changes in the prices and quantities of commodities in the event of changes in the larger economic environment. Problems, such as they are, are not so much with the theory itself, or with what it sets out to accomplish. On the contrary, the problem is that this theory, which was developed to understand markets for simple consumer goods, is often deployed to explain and validate the market price of virtually anything bought or sold in almost any kind of market and almost any kind of circumstance. Such efforts are erroneous applications of this theory that merit the criticism they have drawn from economists and the public.

The primary economic argument for deregulation, privatization, and commodification has been the often-repeated mantra that the "free" market has been "proven" to be an efficient means to allocate goods and services.[12] Clearly such a claim is closely linked to the idea – again, one initially borrowed from engineering – that negative feedbacks are ubiquitous in free markets. When American economists or opinion page writers tell us that they "believe in the market," what they are asserting is a belief that negative feedback systems are close to ubiquitous in social and economic systems.[13] Such an assertion is, of course, interesting and important. But it is also one that is, or should be, subject to examination, discussion, and refutation.

A POSTSCRIPT: "NATURAL MONOPOLY"

Before closing this chapter a few observations should be made concerning the production of commodities that involve substantial upfront investments before any revenue can be earned. Consider a production process that requires substantial fixed investments or development costs before it is possible to produce goods or services that are ready for sale (a railroad or a new automobile). As a consequence of this cost structure, the first unit of output is prohibitively expensive. Typically, unit costs fall quickly once the initial production process has been put in place (new software is the quintessential example of this kind of cost structure – developing the first unit can cost tens or hundreds of millions of dollars, while the second can be produced at the cost of mailing a disk or sending the program over the internet).

For commodities featuring the above production qualities the marginal cost of the second unit of production is substantially lower than the first, and the average cost of supplying additional units of the item to the market decreases as the quantity supplied increases. In graphical terms the supply curve will not look like the one drawn in the figures above, rather it will slope downward to the right. This case, while not developed here, is important because it represents a situation wherein an early entrant to the market can stake out a commanding position. The reason is that the costs of the first firm in this market will fall rapidly. These early firms will have the advantage of working with average costs substantially lower than any market entrant can hope to achieve for some time. In business schools and on Wall Street, this is called a "first-mover" advantage. When the production process of a commodity exhibits such a cost structure, and many do, new entrants will face substantial costs and risks which are at variance with the "zero entry costs" conventionally assumed for a perfectly competitive market. New entrants will be discouraged unless they, and the banks backing them, can afford large upfront expenses. These expenses must include what can reasonably be assumed to be substantial losses for an extended period.

When the conditions of supply resemble this case, the industry is said to feature a "natural monopoly." This would be an unimportant addendum to the theory of commodity markets, except that we often find such cost structures in critical sectors such as transportation or communications. In these industries, the existence of natural monopoly was once, some decades ago, considered a *prima facie* case for either public ownership or their treatment as "public utilities" subject to price regulation. By contrast with the political economy of the Progressive Era, over the last 30 years the United States has been remarkably tolerant of such monopolies (Lynn, 2006). Our collective experience with deregulated electricity, airlines, and telecommunications all suggest that we need to rethink our current policies.

NOTES

1. Metaphysical has come to be a term of disparagement among economists and other social scientists who wish to be seen as "scientific." This is a mistake. Here, it is being used in its original sense of referring to concepts that are important to the structure of our ideas and that we believe do exist, but that are necessarily beyond our powers of direct observation. As David Hume once argued so convincingly, ideas of cause-and-effect are, in this sense, metaphysical.

2. "It is not from the benevolence of the butcher, the brewer, or the baker that we expect our dinner, but from their regard to their own self-interest. We address ourselves, not to their humanity but to their self-love, and never talk to them of our own necessities but of their advantages" (Adam Smith, 1776 [1937], p. 14).

3. I wish to reemphasize that in this lecture "commodity markets" does *not* refer to either the spot or futures markets for bulk primary goods, such as the Chicago Board of Trade or the New York Mercantile Exchange. Structurally, these markets are more accurately classified as asset markets, which are the subject of Lecture IV.

4. Economists often express this last assumption by proposing the counter-factual notion that people exclusively derive something they call "utility" through their direct relationship to a product, and for that reason, utility can not be interdependent between people. For example, it is supposed that I will not be happier wearing blue jeans just because you are wearing them, or vice versa. While this assumption supports certain methods and conclusions of mainstream economics, it clearly leaves a lot to the side. For example, fashion, fads, and almost everything that we might term a "culture" become incomprehensible once we buy into this somewhat solipsistic vision of consumer satisfaction.

5. This formulation of the theory of demand was subjected to an important, and unjustly ignored, criticism by Oscar Morgenstern (1940).

6. The prior phrase is in Latin, and hence it appears that much more authoritative. Using Latin in this context is important as it validates the several grade school years I spent studying the subject.

7. The idea that the production process for consumer goods features decreasing returns (increasing marginal costs), and the theoretical, empirical, and policy implications of this assumption have long been subject to serious debate. Since these are elementary lectures, the following references to the literature will have to suffice (Sraffa, 1926, Lester, 1941, 1947; Prasch, 2007). See also the postscript to this lecture.

8. Beginning in the 1960s, the term "political economy" took on an implicit interpretation as a politically "left" perspective on economics. That is not how I am using the term here. Rather, I take it to identify the issues at the intersection of political and economic theory.

9. Just to clarify the terminology being used here, a "stylized fact" is a generalization. It does allow for exceptions. What is being asserted is that history and experience largely support the characterization of causation or fact being put forward.

10. Indeed, this quality of volatility is one among several reasons why Third World countries depending upon the export of primary products to earn the foreign exchange they need to meet their international debt obligations so frequently run into difficulties. The "solution" has been to bridge shortfall periods with lending underwritten by private banks and international development agencies. This lending is often conditional on the receiving nation placing an even greater emphasis on exporting its way to economic growth and specifically relying on those items that the IMF and World Bank consider to be that nation's "comparative advantage." In practice, this often leads to an ever greater dependence on exporting primary products and low-wage manufacturing. A less diverse economy means ever-greater exposure to price fluctuations and more dependence on international financial markets. Not surprisingly, these cycles of boom, debt, and bust are often repeated.

11. A reasonable question is whether such coordination could be difficult, even impossible, if people trade at "false" (non-equilibrium) prices. Investigating this nontrivial question was once an important research project in economics (Hicks, 1939, ch. 9 Appendix; Clower, 1965; Barro and Grossman, 1971; Leijonhufvud, 1981).

12. In not a few cases government officials have supported privatization as a useful way to circumvent rules concerning government transparency. Private firms do not have the same "daylight" requirements that government agencies and, to some extent, the military has. For example, if the executive branch of government wishes to participate in a conflict in Columbia, but would rather not have newspapers or the Congress discuss this decision, it could deploy what are today called "private contractors" (formerly known as mercenaries) to fly surveillance, locate enemy forces, direct local forces into a field of battle, etc.

13. My colleague at Middlebury College, David Colander, makes a valuable distinction between "market failure," wherein it is supposed that the market is failing to work, and "failures of the market," which term he uses to describe cases in which the market is working very well, but to an end or objective that we find pernicious. For example, ante-bellum American slavery would be classified as a case of the "failure of the market" rather than "market failure" as the market for slaves functioned all too effectively.

PART II

Market processes when information matters

LECTURE III

Credit markets: the economics of a "relational" contract

Considered as a market transaction, credit has several distinct properties. Collectively, these are of enough consequence that the market for credit constitutes its own "ideal type" meriting an independent examination. The place to begin is by revisiting a crucial, if often implicit, assumption underlying the analysis of the market for commodities – that these are exchanges of inspection goods in a "spot" market.

To review, in a spot market the transaction is negotiated and settled during a single meeting or interaction. The previous example was a suburban yard sale. There goods are inspected, prices negotiated, and cash tendered and accepted – all in the course of single meeting. Buyers and sellers neither require nor desire the identities, backgrounds, or references for the individual or individuals with whom they conduct such exchanges. To reiterate, such "spot" transactions are the implicit model underlying the textbook theory of supply and demand.

Credit transactions are, and by their nature must be, qualitatively different from the spot transactions that typify commodity markets. When a person or firm enters into a loan contract, they are committing themselves to an ongoing business relationship with another person or institution. Moreover, a loan is not an "inspection good" as one cannot know at the outset if one will be paid back. The lender, who above all wishes to see their money again, is shouldering the risk that this may not occur. For this reason they are necessarily interested in the background, character, and credit-worthiness of the person or organization that is the counterparty to the loan.

But they are not alone in being interested in the qualities of their business partner. The borrower will also be interested in the terms and conditions associated with repayment, renegotiation, and other contingencies that may emerge over time.[1] The "arm's length" relationship through which we exchange inspection goods in a spot market, where names and previous business performance mean little or nothing, fails to depict critical aspects of the market for credit. The reason is that the character and quality of the person or institution with whom one is entering into a loan contract are of non-trivial importance to both parties.

Agreements such as a credit contract, in which two parties have entered into a business relationship expected to persist over an extended period of time, are called "relational contracts." In our contemporary economies most important transactions are relational contracts. When an automobile company enters into an agreement with a subcontractor, a parts supplier, or a major labor union, they are establishing the terms and conditions under which they will purchase parts, inputs, or labor over a multi-year period. This business relationship is governed by a relational contract. Individuals also enter into a relational contract when they agree to rent a home or purchase heating oil for delivery over the course of the winter. Credit is only a subset, albeit a most interesting subset, of the large number and variety of relational contracts that exist in our society. It follows that if we are to understand modern markets it is essential that we develop an appreciation and understanding of the unique qualities of such contracts (Llewellyn, 1931; Macaulay, 1963; MacNeil, 1974, 1978).

Now, if a firm or an individual is involved in a relational contract it should not be assumed that they have decided to eschew, or in any other way neglect, their own self-interest or desire to maximize profits. What is true, however, is the generalization that once a business or a person has entered into a relational contract their self-interest may dictate that it would be unwise to attempt to "get over" on one's counterparty on each and every occasion that arises. A fuller and deeper understanding of self-interest suggests that each partner to the contract will perceive that their long-term interest may lie in cultivating the trust and continued goodwill of their counterparty. This trust will enhance the success and ultimate value of the mutual project, and the business arrangement itself, so that each of the involved parties may continue to participate in an ongoing and mutually beneficial enterprise. But clearly the conditions for this to be true vary from project to project and contract to contract. When discussing incentives under a relational contract, the details are of the most importance.

Indeed, even when each party can perceive the advantage of a successful ongoing relationship, it would still be incorrect to infer that strategic behavior ceases to play a role in relational contracts. Over the last 30 years the economics literature has come to acknowledge that relational contracts, including debt contracts, routinely involve situations of what is called "asymmetric information" (Stiglitz and Weiss, 1981; Stiglitz, 1987). This term is meant to capture the idea that many contracts involve less than perfect information. Of most importance, one or both parties may have what is, in technical jargon, termed "non-public proprietary information" that would be of interest to their counterparty. The side with this information may, but most often may not, find it in their interest to divulge it to the individuals or organizations with whom they have entered into a relational or credit contract. For example, you may have been tardy with several loan payments in the past, and might not wish to share this information with the bank with whom you are negotiating another loan. Your bank, on the other hand, may be in the habit of routinely raising interest rates on customer loans to extreme levels in the event of trivial violations of the terms of the agreement. Or they might be excessively difficult to contact on the telephone. The bank is unlikely to divulge this information to customers with whom they are negotiating. In each of these instances information that is relevant to the negotiation could be profitably misrepresented or withheld.

Withholding crucial information and then using it to one's business advantage after a contract has been negotiated is, regrettably, an all-too-uncommon occurrence.[2] The fact that such behavior routinely occurs raises the cost of doing business and therefore increases the *a priori* cost of transacting. The consequence is to reduce the total number of transactions. Imperfect information means that prudent persons are obliged to undertake costly precautions to protect themselves from unknown or unforeseen mishaps. At a minimum each party will have to spend time, money, and effort gathering information before entering into a loan or other relational contract. Knowing that they do not know, and cannot trust, their counterparty, some people will avoid entering into relational contracts altogether. They would rather get along without certain business relationships, and the benefits they might provide, than accept risks they can neither quantify nor estimate with a sufficient degree of precision.

Businesses, who are working repeatedly with a large number of relational contracts, now routinely contract with outside "databrokers" and other professionals to evaluate the potential risks of counterparties. In this case the major asset of agencies that rate corporate bonds or private individuals, such as Moody's, Standard and Poor's, Experian or Equifax, is their reputation for a fair and dependable assessment. For this service they can charge a fee. The revenue of such firms is, of course, conditional on the value of the average contract that clients are negotiating, and the perceived cost of error to those clients. Since the cost, to a corporation, of error in misrating a potential merger partner is greater than that from misrating a single customer, it should not surprise us to learn that there is substantially more erroneous information in the rating of individuals than of corporations. But for a variety of reasons it would be unwise to believe that this task is being done very well in either sector.[3]

An implication of "asymmetric information" is that its presence can contribute to a problem known as "moral hazard." This term, which originated in the insurance industry, considers that the incentives faced by a counterparty are often changed by the fact that they have entered into a contract. An example of moral hazard might be the shopkeeper who is less attentive to fire safety after paying for fire insurance. The "stylized fact" is that people with insurance, relative to the uninsured, feel more comfortable "cutting corners" or postponing needed repairs. The extremes – and we know that these occur with some frequency – are those instances in which business or home owners deliberately set fires, or arrange for others to set fires, so as to claim the ensuing losses from the insurance company. Such extreme instances of moral hazard are, of course, punishable under the law as arson and fraud. While statistics affirm that such outcomes are fairly common, it is often difficult to gather enough evidence to achieve a conviction.

Another problem associated with asymmetric information, one aggravated in the case of relational contracts, is that of "adverse selection." This is said to occur when a business or organization offers a contract that disproportionately attracts undesirable counterparties. For example, stock-brokerages may disproportionately attract employees who enjoy risk-taking and gambling. More immediate to the subject of credit is the fact that dishonest, desperate, and irresponsible people are more likely than the population at large to borrow money at high rates of interest rates. The famous Scottish economist Adam Smith, among many others, has commented upon this tendency:

> If the legal rate of interest in Great Britain, for example, was fixed so high as eight or ten per cent., the greater part of the money which was to be lent, would be lent to prodigals and projectors, who alone would be willing to give this high interest. Sober people, who will give for the use of the money no more than a part of what they are likely to make by the use of it, would not venture into the competition. (Smith, 1776 [1937], p. 339)

The underlying problem is the reduced average quality of the mix of potential borrowers remaining in a credit market featuring high rates of interest. Smith's belief was that banks would be tempted by these high rates of interest to overlook the changing mix of people willing to take out loans. His concern was less for the irresponsible bank, but rather for the tendency for one bank failure to cast doubt on the reputation of nearby banks, thereby contributing to a potential crisis within the broader financial system.

For the reasons summarized above, bank loan officers, and those who regulate them, may wish to limit their risks by refusing loans to some, even many, otherwise willing borrowers. In economic terms, this means that at the "market rate of interest" the demand for loans will become greater than the supply. In the jargon of technical economics there is said to be an "excess demand" for loans.

Moral hazard and adverse selection collectively lead to the "stylized fact" that, beyond some threshold level, banks and other lenders may be unwilling to supply additional credit as the rate of interest rises. This is not true across the full spectrum of interest rates. Up to this threshold point higher interest rates induce greater supplies of credit. However, as interest rates rise beyond it, banks and other lenders will be increasingly concerned with the underlying character, judgment, and viability of those customers who remain willing to borrow. Even if we could know that all of them are honest and well intentioned, as rates rise borrowers' monthly payments will be larger, which in itself will increase rates of default. The reason is that high interest payments increase costs. As such they reduce the profitability, and thereby the viability, of firms. In sum, the riskiness of any given portfolio of loans rises as rates of interest rise. These considerations are represented in Figure III.1. It captures, from the lenders' perspective, the relationship between the rate of interest charged and the expected return on a dollar loaned. For the reasons

Expected returns per $ loaned

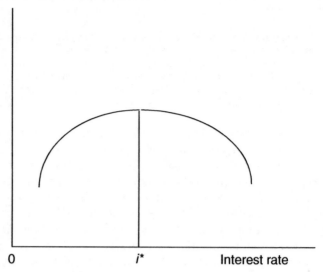

0   *i**   Interest rate

Figure III.1 Expected returns/interest rate relationship

presented above, there is a rate of interest that maximizes the expected return.

At rates of interest rise above $i*$ the expected return on the portfolio of loans declines, and declines at an increasing rate. The reason is that as the rate of interest charged increases, the quality of loans in the portfolio declines and the expected amount of losses from defaulted loans rises. While the bank earns a greater return on those loans that are paid back, it also experiences increased losses from defaulting loans. The above relationship suggests that banks will become more selective in making loans as rates of interest rise above $i*$.

With the above considerations in mind, we can draw a schedule depicting the supply of credit. It is drawn from the perspective of lenders since they are the ones actually or potentially extending loans. Of interest here is that this schedule is "backward bending" at higher rates of interest. This eventuality is illustrated in Figure III.2.

To interpret this Supply of Credit schedule, consider the following scenario. At higher interest rates, many of the people that Adam Smith once described as "sober and industrious" will decide to forgo borrowing. If possible, these potential borrowers will take their

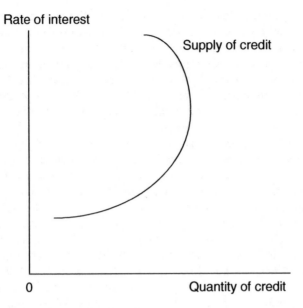

Figure III.2   The supply of credit

business elsewhere. Alternatively, they will forgo the project that was motivating their desire to borrow. Either decision is most sensible. But the explanation is not yet complete. From the perspective of the bank, and that bank's regulator, it is necessary to reflect on the qualities of those persons and businesses that remain in the pool of potential borrowers. Introspection and experience each suggest that those who are dishonest, desperate, or overly optimistic, are less likely than their peers to drop out of the loan market as interest rates rise. Each of these borrowers represent a poor credit risk.

Let us consider, in turn, each variety of potential borrower. If they are dishonest, that is to say they are frauds, they are planning to "skip town" with the money soon after the loan is made. Perhaps it is obvious, but it needs to be stated, that high rates of interest will fail to discourage fraudulent borrowers. The second category is made up of borrowers who are honest and well intentioned, but desperate. By definition desperate people lack good choices. People without good choices are, sad to say, likely to be poor credit risks (There is an old banking adage that says, "Do not lend to anyone who needs the money"). Finally, we have that subset of potential borrowers who are overly optimistic. Such optimists believe that their business prospects are so certain and so remunerative that even high-interest loans cannot present an obstacle to what they believe is their "assured" success. They could, of course, be correct. But, even more often, they are not. In any of the above instances, the fraudulent, the desperate, and the overly-optimistic, banks and their regulators are well-advised to be wary. The history of banking, especially over the past 30 years, reveals that this has not always been the case.

We should not leave this topic before reviewing the likely effects of higher interest rates on the quality of the loans themselves, even if we make the extreme and unlikely assumption that the mix of actual borrowers remains constant. Suppose the identical set of customers all borrow the same quantity of money after interest rates have risen. The probability of default must rise. The reason is that higher rates represent higher periodic loan payments and thereby higher financing costs to firms. After the increase, all firms will experience lower profits. *Ceteris paribus*, lower profit margins mean that all firms will be more vulnerable to the routine mishaps or setbacks that can occur in any business or industry. If we assume some sort of "normal distribution" of returns to business, it will be evident that with higher interest rates more firms will fail, and others will begin to struggle. In the event of higher rates of interest, and therefore higher business costs and less profits, those firms who are in the "lower tail" of an otherwise normal distribution of profitability over any given period will be more likely to face bankruptcy. As Adam Smith and Joseph Stiglitz have each observed, high interest rates disproportionately increase credit risks. This, by itself, can reduce expected revenues and give banks an additional profit-oriented reason to turn down loans to individuals or firms who would otherwise be willing to borrow at unusually high rates of interest (Stiglitz, 1987, pp. 17–20).

In light of the above it is plausible that once interest rates achieve a critical level, and depending upon circumstances this could be a rather high level, the supply of credit may be reduced even as the real rate of interest continues to rise. This possibility is illustrated in Figure III.3, which combines the supply of credit schedule from Figure III.2 with a demand for credit schedule (this latter takes on an appearance similar to that of the demand curve for commodities, with lower interest rates correlated with a higher quantity of loans demanded). We assume that there has been an increase in the demand for credit that shifts its schedule from D1 to D2. As drawn, this higher rate of interest

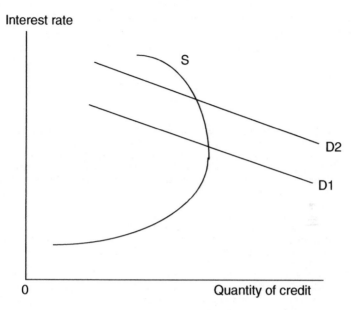

Figure III.3   The credit market with an increase in the demand for loans

increases the revenues accruing to banks, but it is also consistent with a modest reduction in the volume of loans outstanding. However, we would need to know more about projected bankruptcy rates, the overhead costs of banks, and the cost of funds, to know if the banks were eventually better or worse off for this experience.

Unfortunately, even prudent business decisions on the part of banks can have detrimental effects on the larger economy. Consider what occurs when the "real" economy of this region or nation is having difficulties – whatever its ultimate cause. With a recession, the profitability of the system as a whole is brought into question. Prudent banks may experience an increased demand for loans on the part of nervous or struggling firms. Yet, the weakened condition of firms may induce prudent banks to deny loans, even to customers who were previously judged to be eligible borrowers.[4] Such a situation, conventionally known as a "credit crunch," places additional pressure on the economic system by diminishing the amount of cash and loan credit available for business purposes. By denying credit to businesses, prudent financial sector decisions may amplify problems in the larger economy with detrimental and even lasting "real" effects. Many economists and bankers have attributed the severity of the 1991 recession to such dynamics.

NOTES

1. For several studies into the effects on a bank's long-term profitability from building a large, trusting, customer base in the market for credit cards see the several articles by Frederick F. Reichheld (Reichheld and Sasser, 1990; Reichheld, 1993).
2. While this is not the place to develop this point at any length, one of the more striking trends of contemporary business practice has been to enter into relational contracts with customers and then aggressively pursue short-term strategies with the aim of maximizing short-term profits. Thirty years ago business, especially larger businesses, placed a higher value on longer-term strategies directed at growth and market share, and for that reason made significant investments in customer service. After three decades of emphasis on "shareholder value" and "quarterly targets" short-term profit maximization is virtually the only consideration. Such a reconfiguration of business practice brings to mind an earlier and once-eclipsed variety of capitalism – one that was so ably described by Thorstein Veblen over one hundred years ago (1904). Personally, I find the term "Got-ya capitalism" to be useful for describing the increasingly-conventional business practice of punishing trusting or otherwise naive customers.
3. I cannot pass by this issue without observing that it is the height of arrogance that the agencies that rate individuals will "allow" us, often for a fee, to access our own credit reports for the purposes of correcting them! In this manner they charge us to do their clerical work. Since few of us have ever granted permission, or expressed a desire, to have these private sector firms gather sensitive and personal information about each of us, I do not believe that it would be overly onerous to place the burden of accuracy back upon them. To achieve this, consider a law requiring them to pay $100.00 for every error on every credit report they send out and for every instance of unauthorized access. Since a threat to their profitability is the only morality they acknowledge, such a law will likely dramatically enhance their interest in the accuracy and accountability of their work. If it turns out that these firms cannot comply with such a law and stay in business, I would conjecture that few of us would miss their "services." Perhaps we could return to the older (and recently-revived) practice where only our government spied on us?
4. Some depictions of this process have banks maintaining a below-market rate of interest and simply turning away a large number of applicants. The effect is an "excess demand" for loans at this below-market rate. The graph in the text presumes that the cost of funds to the bank has also risen, and that they are following a simple "mark-up" rule in determining the rates they charge their customers, but the "backward-bending" supply schedule indicates that they are extending fewer loans.

LECTURE IV

Asset markets: market dynamics when expectations are a consideration

Financial assets are intangible claims on a future stream of earnings. Examples include stocks, bonds, foreign exchange holdings, etc. Assets are distinct from commodities in that we cannot directly use or consume them. Tangible, as opposed to financial, assets include such delightful objects such as fine wine or rare paintings, are useful in consumption or display, but the market for such items is rather different from that for financial assets. The point is that financial assets have no direct application in consumption as they cannot satisfy a need or a want. Rather, they represent claims on wealth, that is to say they are claims on future purchasing power (of course, the anticipation of future wealth has an impact on current consumption, but that is not the subject of this lecture). To sum up, an asset is a claim on a future stream of revenue (that might or might not take the form of a single lump-sum payment) in the event that a previously agreed upon set of conditions and qualifications are met.

The reason we purchase an asset is because we believe, in light of our expectations at the time of purchase, that it represents the superior flow of revenue based on our collective estimation of the influence of such variables as liquidity, the rate of return and riskiness of other assets, the riskiness of the asset, and how this asset changes the risk profile of our overall portfolio of holdings. The crucial point is that the value of assets, by contrast with commodities, are determined by market participants' collective assessment of the likelihood of future events. Such understandings are called "expectations" and they are a, if not *the*, critical element in the market for assets. For this reason, the market for assets should be thought of as constituting its own "ideal type."

As the reader may have already surmised, the problem is that our assessment of an asset's value is based on a number of uncertain factors, including the interactions between the collective expectations and the most probable actions of other market actors. The inherent uncertainty of the future, conjoined with the inherent uncertainty of human behavior, especially when acting in crowds, ensures that this uncertainty will always be present. This reality reduces the predictability of asset markets, thereby raising the question as to how effective these markets are at their socially-sanctioned tasks. This is particularly the case if an otherwise meaningless change in some minor circumstance or condition induces a cascade of actions that, through a positive feedback mechanism, modifies the structure and stability of market expectations. This, in turn, can reconfigure the quantity and allocation of finance and ownership claims across the society. If this is the case, even a relatively meaningless event can substantially revalue an entire class of assets such as stocks, bonds, or a nation's currency.

THE STRUCTURE OF TIME AND THE FORMATION OF EXPECTATIONS

As previously noted, a critical characteristic of assets is that people and institutions rarely desire them as an end in themselves. The reason is that one cannot use assets, such as stock or bonds, in consumption. They are even useless for conspicuous consumption. It is not an accepted practice to display one's portfolio of stocks on a T-shirt or in any other location where the public could see it. With the exception of misers, few people have a demand for wealth-in-the-abstract. However, it must be allowed that the efforts of some of the super-rich to become ever-wealthier does cause one to ponder the ultimate source of their motivation. But I digress.

Another important characteristic of a subset of asset markets, such as certain varieties of stocks, bonds, and the foreign exchange of a few nations, is their high degree of liquidity. This degree of liquidity is an artifact of high volume in conjunction with low transactions costs including insurance, storage, and other sundry "carrying" costs. A high degree of liquidity means that, under normal trading conditions, traders can move their wealth in and out of these assets quickly and at minimal expense. It is important to understand that every person in the market is cognizant of its high liquidity. From this knowledge it follows that the cost to "waiting" for more information, or for price stability to emerge, can be prohibitively high in the event of a sudden and widespread change in expectations. Especially if this change induces a widespread desire to sell. In such a case, the losses associated with hesitation can destroy the fortunes of an individual or a firm, especially if they have outstanding loans secured by assets that are now of substantially reduced value.

Considering the many uncertainties of such markets, and the pace at which these circumstances can change, one does not always have the luxury of considering all angles and implications. For this reason it is not a surprise that many individuals and institutions have adopted "behavioral rules" or "rules of thumb" to guide their decisions. For sophisticated individuals or firms, these rules may be highly mathematical – perhaps even programmed into computers. At times, these rules of thumb have played a critical role, even a more critical role, than the slower and more deliberate process of estimating "fundamentals." For example, "Diversify" along with "Buy quality stocks and bonds for the long haul" are rules often recommended to those saving for their own retirement or their children's college education. Ideally, such an approach would be taken by their company's retirement plan. "Chartists," the traditional term used to describe those attempting to discern patterns in past market activity, have developed and are continuing to develop, new and undiscovered trends from which to profit.

Casual observation affirms that many firms and individuals practice the relatively simple rule of buying when they see a rising market, and selling when they observe a falling market.[1] When such a "rule" is pursued by a significant number of brokerages, banks, and individuals, the market begins to exhibit a positive feedback between changes in the price of assets traded and the level of demand. Momentum could set in so that the demand for assets rises when asset prices rise, and falls when asset prices fall. When any trading rule is followed by a significant portion of market participants, even if that rule is sensible when followed by a few, it may become an additional and independent cause of instability.[2]

To multiply their earnings some firms and speculators "leverage" their holdings. This means that they have borrowed against their initial holding of assets so as to buy an even greater amount. To illustrate the idea of leverage, let us take an example. Suppose that we manage an "aggressive" stock fund with $100 million. Let us further suppose that we retain 20 percent of all profits for our "management fees" which represents, to be sure, a modest compensation for our innate "genius." Now, we could buy $100 million of stock. If it goes up by 10 percent, we have $8 million for our clients and $2 million for ourselves. Not too shabby.

Alternatively, we could take this $100 million in cash, and use it to secure a loan of $300 million (say at 8 percent). Now let us place this entire $400 million in the market. Let us suppose, once more, that the market rises by 10 percent. With interest, we return the $324 million to our lender and the original $100 million to our clients. Now there is $16 million left over with $3.2 million for ourselves and $12.4 million for our clients. Notice that we have "beat the market" even after accounting for the interest paid because the rate of return in the overall market was 10 percent and our clients received 12.4 percent (12.4/100). Clearly, evidence of our innate genius!

Now, let us suppose that the market declines by 10 percent. The $400 million is now valued at $360 million. The lender to our fund is contracted to receive $324 million, so we must give it to them. There is now $36 million left. Even though our management fees will now be zero, the return to our clients is a loss of $64 million for a rate of return of −64 percent. The point of this example is that a fairly common fluctuation in the market on the underlying asset can induce extremely high fluctuations in reward in the event that investors are highly leveraged. Naturally the sales-side rhetoric of money managers is that upswings are a sign of their genius for management, and declines are simply "bad luck." The point, however, is that genius was never present in this example – only leverage.

The above example illustrates why those whose money is being managed by highly leveraged funds get so nervous during unanticipated price declines. This nervousness can become a demand for repayment. This forces the fund to sell assets, placing further downward pressure on asset prices, which induces others to demand repayment, causing others to sell assets, and so forth. Those who have loaned to highly leveraged funds also become nervous as they may understand how quickly such a fund's assets can evaporate, and do not wish to be left "holding the bag." In such an event, prices can fall a considerable distance before the market's collective price expectations can stabilize around a new level or range. If expectations and debt are structured in the manner described above, asset price declines can be both self-generating and self-fulfilling. Leverage, in short, is an important reason why asset markets can be notoriously unstable on the "downside" (MacKay, 1852 [1980]; Minsky, 1986; Kindleberger, 1996).[3]

If we consider the potential for calamity, and the absence of any "anchor" to stabilize the price of any particular asset or class of assets, a curious question arises. This is, as John Maynard Keynes correctly suggested, the reason for the apparent stability of these markets over relatively extended periods. The periodic booms and busts are easy to understand. Of considerably more interest to social scientists are the extended periods of relative stability (Keynes, 1936 [1964], Ch. 12).

An important source of stability is the conventional belief in a set of abstractions labeled "market fundamentals." Once an estimation of these becomes widespread they can act as "focal point" that normalizes the expectations of traders. Since World War II or thereabouts some credit for market stability has to be apportioned to the Federal Reserve System. Wall Street writers and traders have now formalized its support, and have called it "The Greenspan Put." This term suggests, and experience affirms, that when the prevailing level of asset prices are threatened, as a consequence of a crash in another market, or as a consequence of an important bankruptcy such as that of Long-Term Capital Management in 1998, the Fed will bring about a prompt resolution, up to and including a bailout, so as to preserve the stability and integrity of the larger firms and the system as a whole. Such interventions may or may not be wise when considered over the long haul, but the fact that they now-routinely occur undermines the proposition that asset markets are a "free enterprise" affair. Either way, what are conventionally termed "fundamentals" working in conjunction with periodic Federal Reserve decisions have, over the past several decades, served as "focal points" or "attractors" that have materially contributed to the formation or reformulation of stable expectations for a substantial, usually hegemonic, majority of market participants.

ASSET MARKETS IN ACTION: FOREIGN EXCHANGE (FX)

The fall of 1997 was a fascinating and illustrative moment in the history of the world's financial markets. Several East Asian countries that were then (incorrectly) celebrated as models of orthodox economic development strategies, suddenly foundered under the pressure of unexpected and dramatic flight from their asset markets and from their currencies. Following a time-honored script, the "cure" was for the United States Treasury, working in conjunction with the International Monetary Fund, to impose draconian "structural adjustment" programs on these countries. This included reductions in government expenditure, increased interest rates, and general deregulation, all accompanied by a good deal of unsolicited advice on "good economic fundamentals" and the avoidance of "crony capitalism" (With the United States and the Clinton Administration embracing the Dot.com bubble, this latter advice was more of an instance of "do as we say, not as we do").

The general principle underlying this response was, not surprisingly, the presumption that foreign exchange is a tradable good similar to that of "commodities" as described earlier in this book. Once it is assumed that the foreign exchange (FX) markets are orderly and self-regulating, there is no compelling reason for any government or international agency to employ resources to maintain any particular value of any particular currency (The classic exposition of this position is Friedman 1953). Of course, as the reader may have surmised by now, a theme of these lectures is to question such presumptions. The rest of this lecture will argue that some important distinctions exist, and for that reason *laissez faire* may not represent the best approach to managing the world's FX markets.

UNIQUE CHARACTERISTICS OF FOREIGN EXCHANGE MARKETS

The logic underlying the received theory of the market process, which makes that approach so intellectually compelling, is that no single force operates simultaneously on both sides of the market. The decisions of buyers and sellers are thought to be formed independently of each other, the market price, and changes in the market price. Depending upon the market in question, such a presumption may be more or less valid. A place where it is clearly invalid is the market for foreign exchange. A distinguishing quality of the FX market is that several factors operate simultaneously on both its supply and demand sides. This has consequences for the idea of a uniquely determined market equilibrium.

$/euros

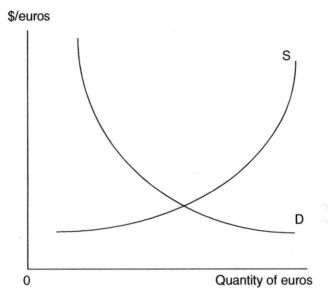

0   Quantity of euros

Figure IV.1   The market for euros

To illustrate the importance of these concerns, let us consider the market for the new European currency, the euro. In this market the demand curve represents the quantity of euros demanded over a given period of time, at a given price, as expressed in dollars. (For purposes of simplification, we are assuming that Europe and the United States are the only "nations" in this market).

The overall demand for euros, which determines the position of the demand curve illustrated in Figure IV.1, is influenced by factors such as:

1.   Expected changes in the $/€ exchange rate;
2.   Changes in the incomes of American residents;
3.   Changes in the relative price level between the United States and Europe;
4.   Changes in the relative expected returns on assets between the United States and Europe;
5.   Changes in the preference for European-made goods by those who currently hold American dollars – typically American residents.

The supply curve represents the potential supply of Euros that will be offered by holders of euros at a given hypothetical price (in US$) over a given period of time. As is the case with demand, the supply curve is subject to changing market conditions. Phenomena that will induce shifts in this schedule include:

1.   Expected changes in the $/€ exchange rate;
2.   Changes in the incomes of European residents;
3.   Changes in the relative price level between the United States and Europe;
4.   Changes in the relative expected returns on assets between the United States and Europe;
5.   Changes in the preference for American-made goods by those who currently hold euros – typically European residents.

The above lists indicate that in the currency markets, domestic incomes and consumer preferences within each individual country are the only independent forces at work. Every other cause operates simultaneously on both the supply and demand for that currency. The implication is that a single cause can induce both curves to adjust simultaneously. Moreover, the presence of price expectations on both sides indicates that a shift in either schedule can be expected to induce a further shift in both schedules. Finally, it is reasonable to suppose that the value of foreign exchange depends on its current and anticipated asset value. In such cases, psychological propensities, including herd behavior, constitute an important aspect of this market (Keynes, 1936 [1964], Ch. 12; Harvey, 1993; Davidson, 1997).

Joint and interdependent supply and demand adjustments in the exchange rate add an important dimension of indeterminacy to this market. The reason is that both sides of the market (current owners of euros and potential buyers of euros) are responding to the same economic stimuli. Moreover, each side is responding to the other side's response to economic events. Actually, they are responding to what they anticipate the other side will do. That, of course, depends upon their expectation of what the first side will do, which depends on what the latter anticipates the former will do, and so on, into an infinite regress. In markets featuring such a structure, it should not be surprising to find that positive feedback loops periodically emerge. The implication is the absence of a determinate result. Equilibria, if they do emerge, cannot be considered unique or stable

(Eichengreen and Wyplosz, 1996). These tendencies are exacerbated by other factors that have not yet been discussed: the role of speculation, and the role of low "transaction" and "carrying" costs.

THE ROLE OF SPECULATION

In the foreign exchange market, as in most asset and money markets, speculators profit by anticipating price changes. To this end, speculators will buy (or sell) a currency if they are convinced that the value of a currency is rising (or falling), and they anticipate that they will be able to reverse their position before favorable price trends reverse themselves (Kindleberger, 1996, Ch. 3). Speculation, it must be stressed, is a process distinct from arbitrage. The latter occurs when a brokerage, bank, or relatively wealthy individual partakes of a risk-free profit opportunity by simultaneously selling an overvalued asset in one market and repurchasing it elsewhere. Time, and the potential for unfavorable changes in the relative value of the asset traded, is not a factor in arbitrage whereas it is an important consideration in speculation. This distinction is important since it is blurred in too many discussions of the speculative process. Worse, speculation may be (incorrectly) presented as another instance of arbitrage. Indeed, one reason for this widespread confusion of terms is that Wall Street "Arbitrageurs" are almost always speculators, but to comfort the wealthy individuals and banks that underwrite their trades, accurate labels are avoided.

The fact that the foreign exchange market is somewhat unstable provides an opportunity for speculation. Under certain conditions, this speculation can contribute to the instability that attracts and rewards even more speculative activity. Such a surfeit of speculation would be innocuous if, like the horse track or the gambling casino, these contests had little or no impact on the "real" economy. Regrettably, we have no such assurance. The reason is that the bulk of the world's trade and international loans are negotiated, contracted, and settled in just a few prominent currencies. Since developments in the foreign exchange market can disrupt other markets, including the markets in stocks, bonds, imports, exports, and many consumer goods, the stability of these currencies can become an important public policy concern.

THE ROLE OF LOW "TRANSACTION" AND "CARRYING" COSTS

Transaction costs are the expenses associated with trading in a particular market. These include the time and costs of negotiating a contract, insuring the shipment of goods, the cost of actually delivering the items to the buyer, etc. Carrying costs are the expenses that one incurs by holding an asset. For example, if one owns a painting by one of the great masters, the carrying costs include insurance, temperature control, the physical security of the painting, etc.

A prominent quality of the major foreign exchange markets is that their transaction and carrying costs are low or negligible relative to most other markets. This is a consequence of their large volumes working in conjunction with modern computerized trading and settling processes and conventions all of which, by design, minimize transactions and carrying costs. The contrast with the markets for shoes or economics books could not be more stark. There are considerable costs associated with entering and leaving these markets. These higher costs are an important reason why less speculative activity occurs in such markets.[4]

Economists have long stressed that people will, *ceteris paribus*, do more of something if it is cheap. Consequently, we should expect ever increasing amounts of speculative activity in foreign exchange markets as transaction and carrying costs decline. Additionally, to the extent that speculation is a normal good, increasingly unequal distributions of income and wealth will contribute to it. For the last several decades it has been evident that the annual quantity of FX transactions swamps any plausible demand that can be attributed to trade, travel, hedging, or other "real" business activities (Ghosh, 1995; Frankel, 1996).

A consequence of the institutional changes that have so profoundly reduced both transaction and carrying costs has been, as was hoped, the generation of an enormous volume of activity in these markets. Another probable consequence has been an enhanced degree of price movement in these markets. Specifically, we now routinely observe price movements that no longer maintain a consistent, or in the short-term even discernible, connection to economic fundamentals (De Grauwe, 1989, Ch. 9; Frankel, 1996).

Volatile FX markets contribute to an increased degree of uncertainty. This generates a number of associated problems. One of these is the increased cost of overseas trade. Those engaged in foreign trade must either accept the additional risks associated with fluctuating exchange rates or purchase hedges in futures markets to guard against them. Other costs that can be attributed to enhanced price fluctuations include the decimation of jobs and industries that occurs when the exchange rate undergoes an extreme appreciation such as occurred during the early-to-mid-1980s. During that period exports were diminished, import competition rose, and firms were obliged to cut their costs and profit margins to defend their market share. Likewise, if the value of one's own currency greatly depreciates, one's trading partners experience a substantial price disadvantage. Tariffs, competitive depreciations, and other trade disruptions are predictable consequences (De Grauwe, 1989, Ch. 12).

To avoid these dilemmas, countries have made periodic efforts to manage or even control the exchange value of their respective currencies. A prominent historical instance was the fixed exchange rate system of the nineteenth century we remember as the gold standard. The gold standard was considered, at that time and today, to be an essential component of the nineteenth century's commitment to *laissez faire* (Clarke, 1988, pt. II; Eichengreen, 1992). The Bretton Woods system of the mid-twentieth century was a deliberate effort to preserve the virtues of fixed exchange rates, while simultaneously attempting to account for the deflationary bias that characterized the gold standard. Given the effort that has been expended over most of the last two centuries to manage or control FX fluctuations, it is almost remarkable to ponder the now-conventional assessment that freely fluctuating exchange rates are best.[5]

TOWARD ORDERLY FOREIGN EXCHANGE MARKETS

A more predictable and orderly market could emerge if we reduced speculation in FX markets (Eichengreen and Wyplosz, 1996; Frankel, 1996; Davidson, 1997). This could be achieved in a number of ways. First, a valuable short-term policy would involve a joint and credible announcement on the part of the world's major central banks that speculative exchange rate movements between and among the most prominent world currencies are a concern. At a minimum such a statement, if forcefully presented, could influence the formation and stability of expectations in FX markets. Indeed, the historical record suggests that credible commitments induce supporting speculative movements (Eichengreen, 1992, Ch. 2).

A second policy would aim for a direct reduction in speculative trading by reducing its profitability. A turnover tax on foreign exchange transactions has been suggested as one way to achieve this end. Interestingly, a "sales tax" on foreign exchange would not have to be large to be effective. Based on the long experience of "stamp taxes" and other charges on various stock exchanges, a tax of around 0.5 percent would discourage traders, especially those that like to change their positions frequently, from making whimsical trades. The idea is that an increased cost of trading would induce firms to make a greater effort to find the correct position earlier (Tobin, 1978; Erturk, 2006).

Simultaneously, 0.5 percent is not so high as to discourage traders from conducting normal business transactions such as hedging against risks incurred in the normal course of international trade in goods and services. If it works as predicted, this small tax will at least partially pay for itself. The reason is that with lower FX volatility, the cost of purchasing a hedging instrument in the markets will also decline, thereby offsetting a portion of the initial tax.

Such a tax can also be expected to enhance the autonomy of central banks. Today, commercial banks, speculators, and other FX traders and brokers know that the overwhelming majority of central banks are working at a disadvantage relative to the size and breadth of the world's FX markets. For most nations, it is prohibitively expensive to engage in meaningful foreign exchange operations. One reason is that under current arrangements virtually all of the risk and potential expense associated with managing currencies is placed on central banks. When speculators are selling the currency, and the central bank purchases in order to prevent a devaluation, speculators trade at virtually no cost. If the central bank cannot continue to purchase and is forced to devalue, speculators reap a significant profit. By contrast, the central bank can only break even if they succeed in preventing a devaluation. Alternatively, they can take a substantial loss if they cannot continue to purchase and are forced to devalue. It follows that speculators are better off, on average, under current arrangements. A turnover tax on FX transactions would partially even the odds.

As with any market in which we wish to reduce the quantity of activity, higher prices should decrease demand. If speculators faced a sales tax on foreign exchange transactions this would, *ceteris paribus*, lower the expected returns and diminish their enthusiasm. Moreover, should it turn out that the central bank succeeds in maintaining a specific exchange rate despite the selling pressures of speculators, the latter would face a loss equal to 1 percent of their total purchases. The reason is that it would cost speculators 0.5 percent to sell or short the currency in question, and 0.5 percent again as they returned to the portfolio they held prior to their effort to profit from a forced or anticipated devaluation. On the other hand, the threat of a broadly-based flight from a currency will continue to exert formidable "market discipline" on central banks since a 0.5 percent tax is inadequate to prevent the selling of a genuinely weak or overvalued currency. Such pressures, even without the assistance of excessive speculation, will remain effective checks on the discretion of central banks.[6]

To summarize, with a modest transactions tax, one not at all out of line with the taxes and fees that were long a fixture of a number of prominent asset markets, FX markets will feature an improved balance of power between central banks and private speculators, less speculation, and more stable currencies. The world, meanwhile, could look forward to a more stable foundation for international trade, and perhaps partially restore a basis for a revival of the growth rates that existed during capitalism's "golden age" from the end of WWII to the demise of the Bretton Woods system (Weisbrot et al., 2001). Granted, some will be disappointed. That list would include the big commercial and investment banks, hedge funds, and other substantial currency speculators. We should expect them, their paid consultants, and their kept intellectuals and lobbyists to resist such prospects.

NOTES

1. In the polite language so emblematic of the Internet Bubble of the 1990s, such traders were called "momentum investors," as opposed to "followers of the herd." Remarkably, firms with names such as Momentum Securities emerged at this time. Apparently this choice of name reinforces the message that investors may be assured that the firm's managers would studiously follow the herd. Suffice it to say that the nomenclature of American financial markets, dominated as they are by the rhetoric of salesmanship, is a subject unto itself (Frank, 2000; Cassidy, 2002).
2. This, in essence, was the problem with "portfolio insurance," that became so widespread in the mid-1980s. Since so many firms had computers programmed to sell under similar conditions, a minor downturn had the potential to become strongly self-reinforcing. On October 19, 1987, it was.

3.   The politics of our era discourages persons of good reputation from admitting this reality in public forums (unless a crisis is undeniably underway). For this reason significant asset-price adjustments must always be attributed to some external "cause" – no matter how implausible. Hence the October 1987 crash was blamed on a modest rise in the interest rate that took place a week or so earlier. What is at stake, of course, is the public's faith in the "rationality" of the stock and other asset markets, and thereby the suitability of these markets for the "efficient allocation of scarce investment capital." If the social value of these otherwise remarkably expensive set of institutions were to be widely questioned, or the whole process came to be thought of as the "by-product of a casino" (Keynes, 1936 [1964], ch. 12), some political pressure aimed at regulating or circumscribing their activities might emerge. Even worse, people might begin to question the legitimacy of the large incomes routinely commanded by the "stars" of Wall Street investment houses, and the wisdom of having the agendas of the nation's major corporations set almost exclusively with an eye to next quarter's stock market price (Lazonick and O'Sullivan, 2000). Since such eventualities are too terrible to contemplate, they remain beyond the pale of accepted and acceptable political discourse. Hence ascribing "rationality" to the stock market remains an important, albeit intensely ideological and political, act.
4.   "Of the maxims of orthodox finance none, surely, is more anti-social than the fetish of liquidity, the doctrine that it is a positive virtue on the part of investment institutions to concentrate their resources upon the holding of "liquid" securities. It forgets that there is no such thing as liquidity of investment for the community as a whole" (Keynes, 1936 [1964], p. 155).
5.   While this chapter cannot accommodate an explanation, I would argue that this change in the conventional wisdom reflects the recent hegemony of the financial sector over the real goods sector of the world economy. While these two sectors are not necessarily in conflict, they do not have identical interests either.
6.   Other scholars have argued that the problem of adverse speculation is so powerful that a good case can be made for more extensive controls over foreign exchange to even more substantially reduce speculation and further enhance central bank independence, but the issues involved are beyond an introductory book (Crotty and Epstein, 1996; Davidson, 1997).

PART III

Labor markets

LECTURE V

Labor market dynamics when needs are a consideration

Labor, that is to say the purchase and sale of a person's capacity to work for someone else, is another exceptional case that motivates at least two "ideal types" of markets. The reason is that labor markets trade a highly unique item – the time and effort of living, thinking, persons. Persons, unlike inanimate objects, have rights, obligations, and needs.

For a moment, let us contrast the exchange of labor with that of a clove of garlic. In the case of a clove of garlic, the transaction can be characterized by the legal condition of being "free and clear" in the sense that after settling with the previous owner I can use the clove of garlic in any manner that I see fit. I might use it to flavor an Italian dish, scare off vampires, or give it to a friend. My use of this clove of garlic is a matter of indifference to the individual or grocery store that sold it to me once its purchase has been negotiated and settled. The reason is that the seller is neither at risk, nor emotionally vulnerable, nor suffers any compromise of their rights, dignity, or any other type of loss no matter how I eventually dispose of this garlic.

The above characterizations do not apply to labor. If I agree to work for a wage, I almost always have to deliver the contracted labor in person. For that reason I remain highly interested in how I am treated at my place of employment. I have every reason to be concerned if my employer decides to put my person at risk, abuse me, or otherwise injure me in the course of completing my job-related tasks. Moreover, certain state agencies and the courts may take an interest in my situation.

But the issue raised in the previous paragraph, important as it is, is just one element of the distinction. As a person I have the ability to *reflect* upon my situation, my actions, and the situations and actions of those around me. From these and other sources, I can derive attitudes and ideas about how I have been treated, or what I have been asked to do. These attitudes and ideas may or may not correspond to those of my boss. Clearly such reflections are beyond the capacity of a clove of garlic. If left by a sunny window garlic will spoil, but it is unlikely to develop a sense of outrage at such negligent treatment.

Additionally, while it is the case that we can purchase the labor power of an individual or individuals, it is another matter entirely to motivate and inspire them to work at a high level, and perhaps even be open to learning new approaches to doing things – new approaches that may, or may not, be usefully deployed elsewhere. In the event that these learned skills can be deployed elsewhere, I may find that I have inadvertently contributed to the capabilities of one of my competitors' employees if my employee is then hired away.

It should now be evident that labor is different from a simple consumer good, such as a clove of garlic, in several meaningful ways. These are qualities that can, or should, matter for economic analysis. This lecture will address only one of these meaningful differences – the role that needs play for the theory of labor supply. The next lecture will address the importance of reflection or self-consciousness in the supply of labor. While other issues exist, they are addressed in more specialized writings (Fine, 1998; Prasch, 2004b).

We begin with a fairly banal observation. This is that labor is necessarily contributed by human beings, and that all human beings can be presumed to have needs. While this analysis is not dependent on any particular list of needs, one might reasonably surmise that such a list would include food, shelter, basic medicine, potable water, etc. But, as will be seen, much follows from this seemingly innocuous assumption. At a minimum, it will become evident that the market for labor must be its own "ideal type."

The crucial distinction is as follows. When the price of a consumer good or commodity falls, the theory of supply maintains that suppliers will substitute out of the business of providing that particular item, and devote more of their productive capacity to the provision of some other item. Broadly speaking such an assumption is both reasonable and plausible, although we can quibble over the size of the adjustment costs. For example, a low price for minivans relative to other large vehicles will induce automobile manufacturers to apply more of their productive capacity to the manufacturing of substitutes, perhaps light trucks or sedans. But can such a line of reasoning be applied to the aggregate labor market without modification?

The "stylized fact" upon which the following analysis turns is that most of us depend upon the sale of our labor for the bulk, if not all, of our income. Stated simply, our livelihoods depend on our labor market earnings. In light of this fact, can we plausibly conclude that lower wages will induce people to "substitute" into leisure and thereby reduce their effort to earn a living? After all, how many people can live off the bounty of the land, depend upon their savings, or count on the beneficence of family, friends, or the welfare state to meet their day-to-day needs? Yet, such a choice is implicit in conventional depiction of the labor supply curve.[1] For the above reason, I would argue that presenting the supply of labor schedule as if it were the supply of any other commodity is an implausible representation of the decision faced by the overwhelming majority of people in the American labor market. It even more completely misrepresents conditions in the Third World. Happily, a more substantive and defensible specification of the relationship between income and labor supply can be constructed without losing the foremost merit of the conventional model – its analytic and pedagogical simplicity.

THE CONVENTIONAL LABOR SUPPLY SCHEDULE

The upward sloping supply curve for what are termed "factors of production" holds a prominent place in textbook discussions of the labor market and, as a consequence, the distribution of income. As one among several productive "factors" the conventional, or textbook, labor supply schedule depicts the quantity of labor supplied as a direct function of the inflation-adjusted wage rate, often called the "real wage." The aggregate labor supply schedule is typically presented as a summation across all of the labor–leisure "choices" made by every actual and potential worker in a given labor market (cf. Katz and Rosen, 1991, pp. 133–50; Taylor, 1998, pp. 326–9).[2]

Despite the apparent consensus at the textbook level, there is some dissatisfaction with the conclusions typically drawn. One is suggested by our actual experience with labor markets. Over the years, numerous empirical studies have indicated that the labor supply schedule is nearly vertical or even sloping downward to the right (Lester, 1941, pp. 104–08; Kaufman, 1994, pp. 60–2; Gordon, 1996, ch. 4; Bluestone and Rose, 1998, 28–30; Dessing, 1999; Mishel et al., 1999, pp. 307–14). If this is the case, then textbook representations of the labor market, specifically the shape of the labor supply curve, have to be revised.

To partially address these empirical concerns, the labor supply curve is sometimes presented as "backward-bending" at *higher* levels of wages. For over 50 years economic theorists have acknowledged that at high wages, and consequently high income levels, the representative worker will wish to purchase more of all "normal goods." Since "leisure" (defined in the broadest sense as doing anything but working for wages) is a normal good, high wages can induce a reduced quantity of labor being supplied to the market. Such a modified labor supply curve appears in Figure V.1.

Underlying this result is the plausible notion that "leisure" has properties that mimic those of normal goods. With the increased levels of income that follow from higher wages, people will wish to "purchase" additional units of "leisure." This tendency is known as the "income effect." But, we also have to consider another consequence of higher wages – we can purchase more of all things. It would not be sur-

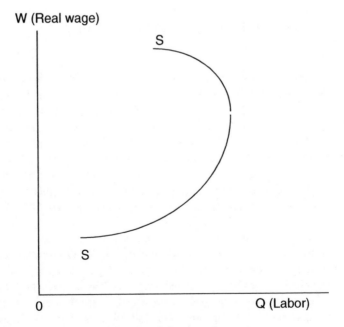

Figure V.1   Backward-bending labor supply curve

prising if some of these items are desirable enough to induce us to work a bit longer at our high wages. It follows that high wages also induce a second tendency that is in opposition to the income effect just described. This is a tendency for higher-compensated workers to "substitute" out of "leisure" time into additional labor time. This "substitution effect," like the income effect, is a plausible response to higher wages.

The substitution and income effects, although pressing in opposite directions, are each consequences of a single cause – higher wages per unit of time. In technical language, economists have agreed on the "stylized fact" that there exists some relatively high wage that enables the "income effect" to dominate the "substitution effect" (*ceteris paribus*, of course).

Despite these theoretical propositions, an additional problem remains. The labor supply schedule depicted in Figure V.1 suggests that, as wages decline below some point, the quantity of labor supplied will steadily decrease. Yet empirical studies consistently fail to support this formulation. The American experience from the 1970s to the mid-1990s, which featured a conjunction of falling or stagnating wages and increased work hours for the bulk of the population, fails to support such a depiction of the labor supply schedule (Schor, 1992, chs. 1–3; Gordon, 1996, ch. 4; Mishel et al., 1999, pp. 307–14). These tendencies are even more pronounced outside the developed world. In separate studies Maryke Dessing and Mohammed Sharif have each identified similar tendencies across a broad range of Third World labor markets, thereby undermining the idea that the quantity of labor supplied declines as wages decline (Dessing, 1999; Sharif, 2003). This substantial array of facts, considered in conjunction with implausible foundations, suggests a pressing need to reassess and reconfigure the shape of the labor supply schedule.

INCOME AND THE VALUE OF LEISURE

Conventional depictions of labor supply posit a positive relationship between income and the value of leisure. This is plausible as it is consistent with the experiences of the bulk of the, relatively well-off, people who read economics books. It draws its strength from the notion that, as incomes rise, people will place an ever-higher value on an additional hour of time away from paid labor, and that they may even be willing to "purchase" it with a portion of their rising incomes. Implicitly, this theory suggests that while a person with a substantial quantity of leisure may place a low value on additional quantities of it, additional leisure is always and everywhere a good thing. Consistent with its posture toward goods in general, the received theory assumes that additional free time is always better.

Yet in light of what empirical studies suggest concerning low wage labor markets, perhaps this latter assumption needs to be reevaluated. Here it will be proposed that under certain conditions, increased leisure is not only undesirable, but might even be perceived as disagreeable. This, perhaps striking claim, is grounded upon several "stylized facts" that readers may find plausible once they reflect upon the relationship between leisure and income:

1 Leisure worthy of the name is generally a "joint product" of free time and purchasing power. For example, if I enjoy the perfect margarita on my spacious deck overlooking the ocean in front of my Laguna Beach home, my leisure is more fulfilling than if I spend the same quantity of time drinking a cheap beer in a dark, dingy, and cold apartment.

2. In the economics literature, "leisure" is an omnibus term for time not spent working for wages. Often it includes time spent on duties and chores that can more accurately be termed "personal work" (Mincer, 1963; Prasch, 1997). Cleaning the house, paying taxes, and washing dishes all fall into this category. One way to affirm this is to observe that the wealthy and even much of the middle class are willing to pay for someone else to attend to a substantial portion of their personal work. As a consequence, they can devote a larger percentage of their non-work hours to the pleasures that non-economists usually associate with the word "leisure." Indeed, as a partial response to this problem, and as a reflection of the changing distribution of income, we now see the emergence of firms that, for a fee, will attend to the personal work of others (Levine, 1997, pp. 114-18). To the extent that the wealthy can substitute money for personal work, they can derive more utility from their non-work hours.

3. It is a flagrant misuse of language to assert that the destitute individuals living upon the sidewalks of our major cities are "enjoying leisure." For many of the persons who find themselves in such a predicament, additional free time is a burden rather than a boon.

The theme running through the three propositions above is that, at sufficiently low levels of income, the value of additional leisure time can be negative. They collectively suggest that a destitute person spending his or her "leisure" looking for work, negotiating with the bureaucracy of an increasingly intrusive and judgmental welfare state, or listening to their children plead for food, may perceive additional "leisure" hours to be both long and painful.

Of course our conventional understanding, and the received view of labor economists, is that additional leisure "must be" a benefit. Therefore it needs to be repeated, and emphasized, that the generalization made in the previous paragraph is closely grounded upon the three propositions presented above. Consequently it is evident that the conclusion was derived without invoking some concept of "refined taste" or any other aspect of snobbery. On the contrary, the generalization or "stylized fact" being advanced here is that, as a consequence of low purchasing power, the poor face a diminished quality of life during the hours that they are not working for wages. Unable to meet their basic needs, they face such diminished prospects that additional leisure hours may be unwelcome.

REVISING THE LABOR SUPPLY CURVE

If the value of free time is partially a function of income, and low levels of income are incompatible with a decent standard of living, then it is possible that if wage levels decline far enough, economic agents (a person or a family) will be willing to work additional hours. The reason is that the additional income will enable the person (or family) contributing the additional work effort to more fully appreciate the hours of leisure that remain. Graphically, the result is a second "bend" in the labor supply schedule as depicted in Figure V.2. The level of wages at which this lower "bend" in the labor supply curve takes place may be termed, in honor of the classical economists, the "subsistence wage" (W_s).

Despite the above respecification of the relation between wage levels and the quantity of labor supplied, it remains the case that over an extensive range, lower wages will continue to reduce the quantity of labor supplied – as the received theory predicts. This portion of the labor supply curve can be thought of as consistent with the experience and behavior of middle- and upper-middle class Americans.

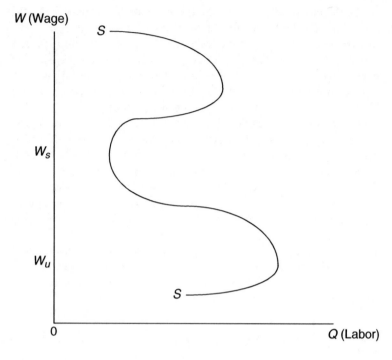

Figure V.2   Revised labor supply schedule

However, Figure V.2 supplements this tendency with the additional proposition that once the real wage (W) falls below the subsistence wage (W_s), the quantity of labor supplied will begin to rise, even as the real wage continues to fall. This trend will continue until the total hours of work required to maintain a socially acceptable standard of living are too long to be sustainable. As a consequence, when the real wage falls so far (to W_u) that the hours that a family must work to maintain its subsistence are simply unsustainable, the hours worked will once again decline, and rather precipitously. The reason is that the primary worker and his or her family will be forced by exhaustion, disease, despair, and disrepair to abandon their effort to maintain a standard of living consistent with effective membership in the labor force and, consequently, civil society. They become homeless, petty thieves, or beggars, with strong prospects for a relatively short and miserable life.

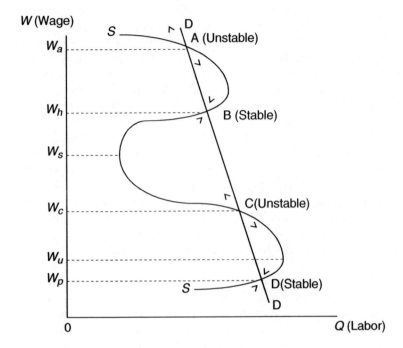

Figure V.3   Revised labor market

MULTIPLE EQUILIBRIA IN THE LABOR MARKET

If Figure V.2 is an accurate reformulation of the labor supply schedule, the labor market may be characterized by multiple equilibria. To illustrate this, let us stay with the conventional representation of factor demand functions and assume that the labor demand schedule slopes downward to the right as depicted in Figure V.3.[3]

If we consider the revised presentation of the labor supply schedule in conjunction with a conventional downward-sloping labor demand schedule, we could find ourselves with a revised graph of the labor market featuring four points of intersection. Two of these equilibria are stable and two are unstable. All four are of interest.

It will be supposed, in keeping with conventional presentations of labor market dynamics, that when the quantity supplied of labor is greater than the quantity demanded, the real wage will fall. Likewise, when the quantity demanded is greater than the quantity supplied, the real wage will rise. With this in mind, and turning once again to Figure V.3, it can be seen that when the market wage is higher than W_a, competitive pressures will induce it to rise. When the real wage is just below W_a, competitive pressures will force it to decline until a new equilibrium is established at point B. It follows that point A is an unstable equilibrium.

Between points B and C, the wage will tend to rise until it is consistent with the equilibrium at point B. It follows that point B is a locally stable equilibrium. Given the stability of the equilibrium at point B, the range of wages between W_s and W_a is consistent with the self-regulating labor market of the textbooks – and the *laissez-faire* policy recommendations that typically follow from those presentations. This explains why the range of wages between W_s and W_a is emphasized in conventional presentations of the labor supply schedule.

Wages below W_s are interesting since they capture some of the novel aspects of the revised labor supply curve. As wages fall below a level consistent with subsistence, continued declines induce a higher quantity of labor supplied as people struggle to maintain a standard of living consistent with the norms and values of their society. However, so long as we remain above the unstable equilibria at point C, the quantity demanded of labor is continually greater than the quantity supplied and there are pressures in the system to return it to the higher wage equilibria at point B. However, at wage levels below W_c, these countervailing tendencies are defeated. The quantity supplied of labor is now greater than the quantity demanded and for this reason market forces will now press wages even lower as people strive to supply ever-increasing labor hours in an effort to sustain a minimally acceptable standard of living. The graph suggests that these efforts will result in a tragically perverse outcome. The willingness of downwardly mobile people to work additional hours places additional pressures on the market wage – which continues to fall – thereby inducing even greater work effort. This process continues until the market achieves another locally stable equilibrium at point D.

Just above the stable equilibria of point D, the market registers its greatest quantity of labor supplied at a wage of W_u. Here the total number of labor hours supplied in the effort to maintain subsistence reaches a level that is unsustainable. Fatigue, disease, despair, and disrepair place an inescapable upper boundary on hours of work. With only 24 hours in a day, the human body can only sustain so much effort. At wages below W_u, people are defeated by their physical and mental limitations. It follows that they are forced to surrender their effort to maintain a subsistence standard of living. The family in question then cuts back on its labor supply. This conception is consistent, to put it dramatically, with dropping out of the workforce. In a country with a welfare state it may be supposed that they turn to its programs for support. Absent formal or informal support, they become indigent and live outside of the structure of society. As mentioned above, they become homeless, petty criminals, beggars, or simply die off.

The larger lesson is that in a free market setting, where people must depend upon their labor to meet their needs, inordinately low wages can continue to decline as a consequence of their previously low level. In such a market, featuring as it does a system of "cumulative causation," low incomes lead to even lower incomes. Stated simply, in a "free" labor market poverty can induce even greater poverty.

Such a theory of labor market dynamics, by contrast with the received view, provides a different perspective on some long-standing labor market interventions, including laws over child-labor, maximum hours, and minimum wages. The concern is to avoid the low-level equilibria, what was once termed a "poverty trap." Prior to our own era, such concerns were better understood. Consider the following observation made almost one hundred years ago by Henry Rogers Seager, a founder of the American Association of Labor Legislation and an economics professor at Columbia University. "Under these circumstances, as our experience abundantly proves, the free play of economic forces results in starvation wages for thousands and hundreds of thousands of workers, and these starvation wages persist year after year, with little or no sign of improvement" (Seager, 1913, pp. 82–3).

In the terms introduced earlier in these lectures, these low-wage dynamics are an example of a positive feedback system, or "vicious circle," at work in the economy (Prasch, 1998a). According to the revised labor supply schedule, market processes can push a perversely low wage rate ever further from the range consistent with a self-regulating market. Wages are relentlessly pressed into a range featuring "destructive competition" among those who must earn their living exclusively from supplying their labor. (Destructive competition was the early twentieth century term for those varieties of competition based on shifting the legitimate costs of production onto others – through degradation of the environment, the labor force, etc.

This concept was to be contrasted with competition driven by improvements in organization, products, or processes.) These dynamics enable us to more sensibly interpret the following statement by labor market reformers John Commons and John Andrews: "Another reason for the low wage scale . . . is the cutthroat competition of the workers for work" (Commons and Andrews, 1916, p. 170).

The novelty of the revised labor supply schedule presented in Figure V.3 is that it features two locally stable equilibrium points – points B and D. These reflect high wages/low hours and low wages/high hours respectively (I will ignore all initial wage levels higher than W_a). Under "free market" conditions the system has a built-in tendency to gravitate to one of these two points and remain there. The particular equilibrium that is eventually achieved is entirely dependent upon initial conditions in the market. This is a critical finding. If this theory is a plausible representation of the low wage labor market it follows that no amount of education, training, exhortation, or lectures on moral uplift directed at the poor will force the labor market equilibrium to move from point D to point B. Once achieving a poverty trap, the system remains there. End of story.

Point D, which is consistent with a wage level below the subsistence wage, is a locally stable equilibrium point as is point B. Given the existence of two locally stable equilibrium points, there is no *a priori* reason to believe that the equilibrium at point D is more "natural," "efficient," or likely to occur than that at point B. Moreover, the wage level at point D can no longer be presumed to uniquely represent the "true market value" or "marginal product" of labor. The reason is that the lower wage/higher hours equilibrium at point D is every bit as consistent with the operations of a free market as the higher wage/lower hours equilibrium featured at point B. Again, let us recall that both equilibria are locally stable which means that once they are achieved, the market embodies no internal mechanism or competitive force that will induce a change in the result.

IMPLICATIONS FOR ECONOMIC THEORY AND POLICY

The revised theory of the labor market presented above, if accepted, has important implications for economic policy. To begin, let us observe that, at wage levels above W_a, the market is dynamically unstable in an upward direction. The quantity of labor demanded will continue to exceed the quantity supplied at every wage level. Since the quantity of labor supplied will continue to fall as the wage continues to rise, no equilibrium will ever be achieved. The theory posits that these high wages will move continuously upward.

At first brush, this story appears to be consistent with the pay of American CEOs since 1980.[4] In such a state of affairs, there is a prima facie case for a progressive income tax on all wages over W_a. Moreover, and despite the touching concern of those associated with the "supply-side" school of economists, it is evident that such a tax will not reduce the quantity of labor supplied by these well-compensated workers. Indeed the above analysis suggests that a progressive income tax would actually increase the quantity of labor available to the market.

Now one might plausibly argue that this model of the labor market is inapplicable to the labor supply decisions of the very wealthy. For one thing, extreme wealth is rarely a consequence of wages. Rather its typical source is as a reward for ownership of stock shares, a form of return that in an era less attuned to the sensitivities of the wealthy was called "unearned income." Another reason, as Thorstein Veblen and others have long observed, is that economic reward plays a diminished role in the economic calculations of the extremely wealthy. Rather, relative income, social status, and rivalry are issues and motivators of substantially greater consequence (Veblen, 1899). In short, Donald Trump did not star in his own "reality" television show because he was worried about making his rent, or because his wealth was inadequate to meet his needs.

A more interesting and significant lesson follows from the co-existence of two equilibria. These have direct implications for the efficacy of minimum wage or maximum hours laws. Consider, once more, Figure V.3. Suppose a maximum hours law were to be imposed that was just below the hours that would otherwise be contributed at point C. In light of the market dynamics illustrated by the arrows on the figure, it is evident that such a restriction would set processes in motion that would continue until the equilibrium at point B is achieved. Interestingly, the initial hours limitation would not be "binding" in the sense that the equilibrium hours worked once all adjustments had occurred would be less than the mandated maximum – a nice illustration of how market forces can interact with legislation to bring about results that are not immediately evident or expected.

Let us also observe that with such legislation a lower quantity of labor will be supplied than would be the case if the system were allowed to remain at the low wage/high hours equilibrium. This consequence, of course, is the traditional worry of opponents of hours legislation. These opponents have repeatedly argued that in free markets everyone is "free" to "choose" the hours they "wish" to supply. Figure V.3 affirms everything they have said concerning the voluntary nature of labor supply decisions. But, when the situation changes, people revise their decisions in light of the new facts. When market dynamics track them into the high wage/low hours equilibrium, people just as freely "choose" to cut back their hours, enjoy more leisure, keep their children in school longer, etc. Figure V.3 reflects these revised decisions. It follows that even though the observed quantity of labor supplied is lower at point B than at point D, it would be *incorrect* to infer that the market features an excess supply of labor. Rather, what is being observed is the common sense truism that when people earn higher wages, they often make different labor supply decisions for themselves and their families. One result may be a lower quantity of labor supplied, *ceteris paribus.*

The revised labor supply schedule implies a similar analysis in the event that a minimum wage is enacted. Consider, again in Figure V.3, a minimum wage set just above W_c. With such a mandated minimum wage, the quantity of labor demanded will be greater than the quantity supplied. The competitive process will then exert pressure on wages to rise until the market achieves the high wage/low hours equilibrium at point B. As with the above analysis of hours laws, the final result is contrary to much of the received literature. This should not surprise us as these results were a consequence of analysing the problem while holding the false belief that labor was a just another commodity – which is not the perspective taken in these lectures.

In Figure V.3, a minimum wage set just above W_c supports a market equilibrium with a wage rate substantially higher than the legislated minimum. Consistent with more conventional analyses, the quantity of labor supplied does decline as a consequence of this legislation. But, and this is important, this decline is NOT a consequence of an excess supply of labor at the new market level of wages. Rather the observed decline in the quantity of labor supplied can be attributed to freely-made, but different, decisions as to how much wage labor the individual (or family) should provide. Again, the legislative details might vary depending upon the particularities of individual nations, institutions, proposed wage levels, etc. What can be concluded from the above is that revising the labor supply schedule along the lines suggested is consistent with the extensive theoretical and empirical research into the behavior of people who depend upon low wage labor markets to earn a subsistence for themselves and their families. For this reason it is a part of our revised understanding of the economics of minimum wage legislation (Brosnan and Wilkinson, 1988; Card and Krueger, 1995; Prasch, 1996, 2000a, 2000b; Glickman, 1997; Carter, 1998; Prasch and Sheth, 1999; Levin-Waldman, 2000; Waltman, 2000).

In conclusion, this lecture presents an implicit critique of the positivist tradition within contemporary economics – a tradition that long eschewed economic theories or models featuring multiple equilibria. In opposition to that tradition, it argues that a theory of the labor market featuring multiple equilibria sheds some important insights on a subject that has long been downplayed. This is the existence of "dual" labor markets, and the ameliorating properties of minimum wage or maximum hours legislation. In this sense the model of the revised labor supply schedule is not identical to, but is broadly consistent with, the literature on what has been termed "the theory of segmented labor markets" (Edwards et al., 1975; Harrison and Sum, 1979; Gordon et al., 1982). In addition, a labor supply schedule that is downward-sloping at lower wage levels is consistent with the empirical generalization that, in the face of a declining or stagnating median wage, many families, in both the developed and underdeveloped worlds, will work longer hours in an effort to maintain their standard of living (Gordon, 1996, ch. 4; Bluestone and Rose, 1998, pp. 28–30; Mishel et al., 1999, pp. 307–14).

NOTES

1. During the years I was in college in Boulder, Colorado, an individual gained some local notoriety by claiming to be a "breath-airian." As such, he claimed that he could survive and be nourished by air alone. To prove his claim, he offered to sit upon a local mountain top in a position of deep meditation for an extended period. Whatever the physiological merits of his claim, it did have the potential to overturn one of the particularities of labor that is critical to this lecture – he had no needs. On the other hand, it might be pointed out that to eliminate needs he had to first achieve a trance-like level of meditation. This implies that he would not have been a particularly useful employee, so maybe even his example does not rescue the conventional approach to labor markets with its presumption that

labor has the ability to fully constitute itself prior to, and independently of, market relations.

2. Presenting the aggregate supply curve of labor as a simple summary of "individual choices" is problematic for a number of reasons. In keeping with the introductory nature of this book, these will be ignored.

3. The "Reswitching Controversy" of the 1950s and 1960s demonstrated that there is no *a priori* reason to believe that the labor demand schedule has this shape. Readers interested in an in-depth discussion of the issues associated with this debate should consult, among others, articles by Geoffrey Harcourt (1972), Pierangelo Garegnani (1990), and Heinz Kurz (1990).

4. I note that it is merely consistent, since this market is institutionally complex. A partial development of the author's views on this subject have been presented elsewhere (Prasch, 1998c).

LECTURE VI

Labor market dynamics when motivation is a consideration

The previous lecture argued that labor features several essential and distinguishing characteristics. These collectively imply that the labor market does not function in a manner that allows for simple analogies to other kinds of markets. By taking such characteristics seriously it was demonstrated that the dynamics of low-wage labor markets are different from those for simple commodities. Moreover, the theoretical modifications that follow are sufficiently important to change our understanding of what constitutes plausible or defensible labor market policies.

One of the new assumptions introduced above was the proposition that most people, lacking the advantages of inheritance or accumulated wealth, must work to maintain themselves and their dependents. As such, most people must enter the labor market to access the income required to obtain those items that are necessary to function in society. As was discussed, in those cases where, for any of a host of reasons, a person or family finds themselves on the margins of the workforce, without savings or substantial employment opportunities, the market can operate in perverse and detrimental ways.

Yet, from the perspective of business accounting, it is equally undeniable that the wages of labor represent a cost. Such a perspective is in clear contrast to that of employees for whom wages represent a clear benefit – their income. It follows that changes in wages have different implications for those on either side of the negotiation.

It is well-known, and no longer denied, that there has been a dramatic increase in social and economic stratification since the early days of the Reagan Administration. A consequence of this is that significantly fewer upper middle class and wealthier Americans have had any direct experience with the low-wage labor market. This lack of knowledge, when considered in light of most people's inclination to assume that their own experiences can be readily generalized, has created a situation in which many Americans have difficulty understanding the choices faced or the decisions made by those living and working in low-wage markets. Neither do they understand its effects on the morale, lifestyle, and outlooks of those consigned to it for any extended period of time. As a consequence the dynamics of the low-wage labor market, and the decision-making of those individuals caught up in it, appear to be idiosyncratic or even perverse to those who have spent their lives in more comfortable circumstances. Over the years these misapprehensions have provided political support for a variety of flawed labor market policies, and not a few poorly-formulated ideas for the "uplift" of those caught up in low-wage employment.[1]

This lecture will, however, set aside these considerations to examine an altogether different aspect of labor markets, one that is more applicable to the non-poor. But, as will be seen, these considerations will further affirm the broader lesson of these lectures that simple analogies from commodity markets to labor markets should be treated with some skepticism. To begin, let us reflect on yet another unique characteristic of people, and consider how this quality might manifest itself in the labor market (Prasch, 2004b).

LABOR EMBODIES THE QUALITY OF SELF-CONSCIOUSNESS

The characteristic that will be emphasized in this lecture is our capacity for reflection or self-consciousness (Frankfurt, 1971). This capacity is, unfortunately, too rarely considered by economists. But neglect does not diminish the fact, affirmed by both experience and introspection, that perceived fairness and quality of treatment on the job can rival monetary compensation in eliciting employee loyalty and effort.

Our capacity for reflection enables each of us to consider, and form judgments, concerning the qualities of our place of employment. Such judgments have implications for how, and even if, we will continue to work at a particular job or location. By contrast, a capacity for reflection is not commonly associated with broccoli, bags of cement, or other marketable commodities. While it would be incorrect to suppose that our capacity for reflection is always or even routinely exercised, ignoring it altogether has left some economic theorists, and even the management of some important companies, subject to some important errors. This becomes most evident in the event that an employer violates one or more widely-held norms of fair play.

Arguably, reflection or self-consciousness is unique to the productive input we conventionally call labor.[2] Certainly broccoli or bags of cement do not develop an aesthetic, moral, or any other attitude or response to how it is treated or believes that it is being treated. A bag of cement will not think it is unfair if it is emptied before another is opened. Broccoli will not feel violated or cheapened if it is given away to someone else. As Alfred Eichner so wonderfully stated, "It is a matter of indifference to the barrel of oil that is sold whether it is used to heat a house of God or a house of prostitution" (Eichner, 1985, p. 79; see also Marshall, 1920, p. 471).

People, on the other hand, generally arrive at work with a more or less developed perspective on what is right or wrong. They also bring experiences, beliefs, and expectations to their places of employment. As a consequence, management must either work with, modify, or confront these norms and expectations. Ignoring them altogether is rarely an option. The reason is that these attitudes will often be reflected in the quality and even the quantity of work contributed by any given labor force. Such considerations explain why management is, or should be, thought of as a art that is substantially more subtle than supply chain management or operations research.

Now, it is well-known that horses, mules, and camels also exhibit the quality of consciousness. They can learn from previous experience and have emotions as wide-ranging as fear, irritation, and affection. But it would be a stretch to argue that they "reflect" on their surroundings or draw larger meanings from what they are asked to do. While I freely admit to being underqualified to hold forth on the origin and exact meaning of reflection in juxtaposition to consciousness, I am confident that most understandings of these terms accept that reflection, drawing as it does on the ideas of learning, context, and time to make judgments, is largely unique to adult human beings (Frankfurt, 1971).[3]

In labor markets, and labor relations within a firm, the fact of reflection makes an enormous difference. For example, in the contemporary United States the broadly accepted cultural understandings that we (too-freely) label "common sense" support the norm of "equal pay for equal work" for all employees of any given establishment. By contrast, a machine or a mule would not object to receiving less compensation for its services than another, identical, machine or mule. People, experience shows, are typically offended by such treatment unless a compelling reason can be presented to satisfy their sense of fair play. For example seniority, additional education, or superior skill are widely considered valid reasons to pay one person more than another even if they work in similar jobs.[4]

Drawing upon such considerations, prominent economists from John Maynard Keynes to Clark Kerr, Frank Pierson, and John Dunlop have emphasized the importance that employees place on their wage relative to others at the same workplace or in the same industry (Taylor, 1957, pp. 3-31; Keynes, 1936 [1964], pp. 4-22; Kaufman 1993, pp. 75-102). These economists built upon the observation that whether or not a person's compensation is deemed satisfactory or unsatisfactory often depends upon the perceived legitimacy of the bargaining process and how much comparable workers are paid. As professional arbitrators and other labor relations experts know, within every firm and even industry there is not simply a wage or an average wage, but a wage hierarchy. This hierarchy, be it formal or informal, simultaneously draws upon, reinforces, and legitimates employee wage expectations. John Dunlop developed his famous ideas concerning "job clusters" and "wage contours" to illuminate these issues (Dunlop 1957). Smart managers know they should avoid disturbing or upending these hierarchies and their associated expectations without presenting their employees with a clear and compelling reason. Arbitrary wage adjustments that ignore the social and firm-level values implicit in an established wage structure can significantly decrease morale. Such a decline, if widely shared, can disrupt the smooth operation of a business. Taken to the extreme, it can lead to work disruptions or stoppages due to deliberate slowdowns, strikes, or other job actions.

The idea that people are beings with a capacity for reflection, and consequently are concerned with their treatment and status at their place of work, suggests a critical role for effective organization and management in economic production. This insight, combined with frustration with then-conventional labor economics as a field of research, contributed to the development of industrial relations as an independent area of scholarship (Kaufman, 1993, pp. 75–102). These insights have also been the basis for pathbreaking studies into the role of organizations in the success of modern economies (Chandler, 1977; Lazonick, 1991).

THE MARKET FOR LABOR AND THE MARKET FOR COMMODITIES

With the above considerations in mind, let us now return to the elementary theory of the market for a simple commodity. However, we will modify it so that it might be seen to apply to labor. To this end, the vertical axis will feature the inflation-adjusted wage, here simply called the "wage," instead of the commodity's price. The horizontal axis will feature the quantity of labor. These modifications are depicted in Figure VI.1.

Once again, let us recall that in these markets the quantity supplied is adjusted through changes in prices (in the case of labor, wages). With a homogeneous commodity, perfect information, and no transactions costs, people will never pay more than the "market price" for

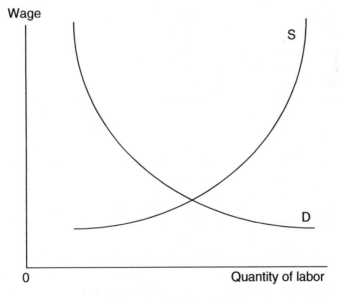

Figure VI.1   Supply and demand of labor (if labor considered as a commodity)

any given commodity. Neither will anyone accept less. Collectively, these assumptions amount to an assumption of perfect arbitrage across the entire market, thereby ensuring all identical items will sell at the same price. In this lecture we will demonstrate that in the case of labor, substantial grounds remain for contesting this proposition, otherwise known as "The Law of One Price."

Now, let us suppose that a firm needs employees to accomplish two distinct tasks. We will further suppose that these employees are identical in every attribute that could be relevant to these tasks. Additionally, we will suppose that neither task has qualities that render it more challenging or difficult than the other, but it will be supposed that the cost of monitoring performance at each one differs significantly.

Let us suppose that the first job can be described as a "staff" task in which monitoring is costly so that the worker has substantial discretion over the speed and intensity of their effort. The second will be supposed to be an "assembly" task that can be monitored at low cost. Should an employee's effort wane while performing this latter task, their "boss" can readily identify this reduced level of effort. Again, recall that we are supposing that all employees are homogeneous. Being of the same innate capacity and ability these employees are paid the same wage. This is, after all, consistent with the principle of perfect arbitrage described above. Here is the problem. If, as is conventionally supposed, there is "disutility" in working, what keeps employees from shirking in their efforts?

Given the structure of the above scenario, it is evident that the employees engaged in the easily monitored task have a direct incentive to maintain their contracted degree of effort. After all, their failure to do so can be readily identified so they risk being disciplined or fired. The reason is evident from the assumptions – it is not particularly difficult for management to ascertain whether or not a given individual is shirking. By contrast, the situation in the "staff" job is neither as simple nor as straightforward. Again, the job task is such that, even in the event of failure, it remains difficult to evaluate the level of effort that was contributed. A wedding planner might be a case in point. The job is not intrinsically difficult, in that it does not require an advanced degree or higher mathematics. But it is hard for a soon-to-be-married couple to monitor the efforts of their wedding planner. Can they be certain that the planner has failed to make a good-faith effort to locate the best and most reliable florist at the lowest prices, found the best caterer at the most competitive price, the most tasty cake, a sober and suitably profound minister or priest, etc.? To an important extent, the couple must place a degree of trust in the proposition that their wedding planner is working as hard as can reasonably be expected.

This leads us to the following interesting possibility. For some types of labor there is an incentive to pay more than necessary, in this case the equilibrium or market wage, in an effort to induce employees to "value" or "appreciate" their job and, as a consequence, contribute a more substantial effort. This tendency, which was once well-understood by economists, was rediscovered a couple of decades ago. Today it is known as "efficiency-wage" theory and has received some degree of recognition (Akerlof, 1982; Shapiro and Stiglitz, 1984; Bowles, 1985). This nomenclature is explicitly designed to evoke the idea that some firms may deliberately "overpay" some or all of its employees in order to enhance efficiency, and thereby lower labor costs per unit of output. In general those who are most likely to receive such a wage premium are employed at tasks where performance or effort is inherently difficult to measure or otherwise ascertain. It follows that paying such a wage premium is not an intrinsically generous act, but rather part of a broader plan to induce greater effort from difficult-to-monitor employees. Again, the presumption is that paying above the existing market wage will induce greater workplace effort and thereby support the firm's most consistent goal – the lowest cost of labor per unit of work accomplished.

While the professional literature advances a host of reasons as to why such a compensation strategy might be successful, only two will be explored here.[5] First, someone paid more than a market wage is earning more and therefore has an interest in keeping such a desirable job. Their self-interest will incline them to more diligently pursue their assigned tasks so as to avoid being caught shirking (while these jobs are difficult to monitor, the probability of being caught is still greater than zero). Second, anthropologists have argued for the existence of a trans-cultural tendency to repay kindness with kindness. For this reason employees who feel trusted and well-compensated are inclined to reciprocate with greater loyalty and effort. The firm "wins" by gaining the benefit of greater effort with lower turnover and training costs. Additional benefits might include a willingness to stay late or come in at weekends to assist in meeting "big deadlines" (Akerlof, 1982).

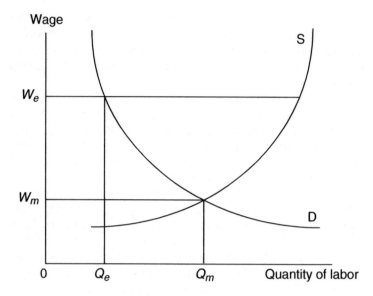

Figure VI.2   The efficiency wage (W_e)

Such considerations, commonplace though they may appear, have enormous implications for our understanding of the labor market. This is illustrated in Figure VI.2. If the above considerations are meaningful, profit-seeking employers would willingly pay an above-market wage to employees engaged in difficult-to-monitor tasks. In Figure VI.2 this is labeled an "efficiency-wage" (W_e). Again, employers willingly pay this premium wage even though they fully understand that other workers of identical ability would be willing to staff these same jobs for the lower, or market, wage (W_m). This tendency, and its effects, are illustrated in Figure VI.2.

In Figure VI.2, and in the absence of the above considerations, the labor market would feature a wage of W_m and a quantity of labor hired of Q_m. But there are other considerations. We are supposing a situation in which it is difficult to monitor the effort expended on some essential job tasks. To enhance efficiency the employer is willing to pay a wage of W_e to at least a subset of his or her employees so that they will value their jobs and contribute a more diligent effort. As can be readily observed from an examination of Figure VI.2, when an efficiency wage is paid, $W_e > W_m$ and $Q_m > Q_e$. It is also evident that at wage W_e more employees are willing to take this job than will be hired. The firm's decision not to hire more people at a lower wage affirms that they believe that they have a compelling reason for not doing so. This is, according to the efficiency-wage theory discussed above, that this task may be more effectively and cheaply accomplished by taking account of employee motivation.

With many otherwise qualified workers now "shut out" of the "primary" labor market, additional numbers of persons will be seeking, and accepting, positions in the "secondary" labor market. (In keeping with a long-standing convention in the economics literature, we will hereafter term the high wage market the "primary" labor market and the low wage market the "secondary" labor market.) Keep in mind that this secondary labor market is exclusively distinguished from the primary market by the existence of a low cost to monitoring employee performance. It follows that paying a wage premium is unnecessary in this secondary market. Given the facts of competitive profit-seeking and rivalry between firms, we can deduce that the market wage will be paid for labor applied to this latter task. This being the case, and in the presence of a now-increased supply of workers seeking work in this secondary labor market, we expect a decline in that market's equilibrium wage. This is illustrated in Figure VI.3.

The increased quantity of labor supplied to the secondary labor market is represented by an outward shift in the supply of labor schedule from S to $S1$. Again, let me reemphasize that in Figures VI.2 and VI.3 we are assuming "homogeneous" labor – that is to say we are assuming that every current and potential employee has equal skills and ability. Nevertheless, in the presence of unequal monitoring costs, the decisions of profit-seeking firms will create a situation of unequal wages and hence a "dual" labor market. To reiterate, the labor market described above is divided *not* according to the inherent ability, capabilities, education, or a superior "work ethic" of one subgroup of employees contrasted with another. On the contrary, the specific qualities of the task assigned are driving the divergence of wages.

The above exposition can assist us in at least partially resolving an apparent conundrum. Why is it that those jobs featuring the best work conditions tend to pay more? In the simple example presented in this lecture, these are the jobs with less direct monitoring. Given that most people do not like to be closely monitored, why is it that in the "real world" additional or even overbearing monitoring is

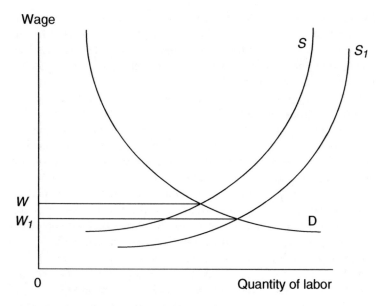

Figure VI.3　The secondary labor market

generally associated with reduced compensation? The reason is that, from management's perspective, paying a wage premium and hiring additional monitors represent alternative strategies (Shapiro and Stiglitz, 1984; Bowles, 1985; Gordon, 1996). From a management perspective, the task at hand is to choose the least-cost approach to maximizing employee effort. In some instances paying more turns out to be the least-cost approach.

Before moving on to the next lecture, it should be observed that the surplus of applicants to the primary labor market is consistent with some important sociological processes that are familiar to all of us. When supply exceeds demand for any given position, employers must establish some criteria with which to choose among otherwise eligible workers. If we consider this fact in a social and political vacuum, it will be evident that employers can set all kinds of criteria for such a selection – including criteria that have no relation to performance. Consequently, a persistent surplus of potential employees hoping for a job paying a premium wage represents an opportunity for an employer to indulge a variety of whims and preferences – even prejudices – in the course of deciding whom to hire and retain. History and experience demonstrate that nepotism, racism, sexism, age discrimination, political affiliation, even a willingness to have sex with the boss, have each and severally been criteria used to select from among a surplus of equally-capable job applicants. Again, with a substantial surplus of eligible applicants, there is no economic "cost" or "penalty" for bosses or their managers to indulge such whims or prejudices.

Workers, who are all too aware that the better-compensated jobs are scarce, know that rewards come from "investing" in any sort of "signal" that might appeal to the moods, whims, or vanities of those employers paying efficiency wages. Sometimes this is close to impossible. Few of us can change our race or gender to suit a prejudiced boss. But other "signals," some of which enjoy wide social approval, do exist. We could, for example, pursue a college education. Selection by such a criteria is acceptable to employers, and upheld by the norms and laws of our society. Given the assumptions of the above model, a college education will have no effect on workplace productivity, but it does provide employers with a non-trivial, but socially and judicially approved, means to select among the surplus of job applicants. Not too long ago, most of the country accepted race and gender as "reasonable" criteria for selecting from among potential employees for positions in the "primary" labor market. When such criteria are widely adopted, dual labor markets serve to reinforce and validate, rather than undermine, pre-existing social prejudices. Today we term such prejudices, when applied to markets, "discrimination." This the subject of the next two lectures.

NOTES

1. This is the origin of the legendary story that had Marie Antoinette exclaiming "Let them eat cake" when she was initially informed that French peasants were without bread. Such a solution would, of course, be plausible for her and everyone in her social circle.
2. Given my seemingly chronic mishaps, I periodically imagine that computers also have a capacity for independent reflection and decision-making.
3. Indeed, it is precisely because children are thought to be lacking a sense of context and a developed capacity for reflection that we do not grant them the legal rights and responsibilities that we conventionally extend to adults.
4. As is well known, for much of American labor history gender or race were widely taken to be valid reasons for discrepancies in opportunity or pay within the same workplace. Happily, these flawed conventions have become less legitimate over the past century (Figart et al., 2002, pp. 16–33).

5. Labor economists will note that in this text I am presenting only two "stories" to
    motivate this theory. As they undoubtedly know, the literature on efficiency wage
    embodies several variants, such as the lowering of turnover and retraining costs,
    the health and stamina of employees, etc. Since this book is presenting the ele-
    ments of economics, and in no way presumes to present a more complete account
    of efficiency wage theory, these two arguments will have to suffice.

PART IV

Social, ethical and political considerations

LECTURE VII

The economics of discrimination: the "Chicago School" approach

Economists have long invoked analogies to the economic theory of commodity markets when examining the consequences of labor market discrimination. This theory of the market, as has been shown above, is constructed upon several important assumptions. Of specific interest to the issue of discrimination, the theory of the "perfectly competitive" market explicitly rejects the notion that distinctions of *theoretical or practical consequence* can be made between different commodities. Arguing from this premise, the "Neoclassical" or "Chicago School" approach to the study of discrimination has long been drawn upon to demonstrate that the "free market" can be relied upon to resolve the effects and thereby the legacies of discrimination (cf. Friedman, 1962, ch. 7; Becker, 1968, 1971; Sowell, 1981a, 1981b).

Crucial to this "vision" are several assumptions concerning adjustment processes. Less clearly defended is the idea that these several assumptions are plausible characteristics of markets as they exist in the real world. If we are to understand the strengths and the weaknesses of the Chicago School approach to the economics of discrimination, readers must remain cognizant of these underlying assumptions. The reason is that they are essential to the construction of the theory, its conclusions, and the policy proposals that follow from it. In short, it is these assumptions that ultimately determine what, from the "Chicago School" perspective, may be taken to be plausible or implausible policies for undermining the consequences and possible persistence of labor market discrimination. As these assumptions are listed, it should become evident that they are similar to the assumptions that characterize "commodity markets" as described earlier in this book:

1. The markets for labor and products feature many small firms, none of which have the capacity to modify wages, prices, or the structure of these markets.
2. An assumption of standardized – literally homogeneous – inputs and final products. For this reason, all current and potential employees are presumed to be identical in every aspect of their ability and motivation. For the purposes of this lecture they can only, and exclusively, be distinguished by their race. (To examine other forms of discrimination, gender, religion, caste, etc., are substituted for race.) It will be assumed that a worker's race can be immediately and costlessly ascertained by everyone in the market.
3. Free and costless entry and exit from each and every market on the part of all firms and employees.
4. Free and costless movement of all other productive resources, including technologies and capital, across all firms currently or potentially in the economy. This implies a perfectly knowledgeable and fluid market in credit. (A critical implication is that everyone, of all races, can borrow money on the same terms at the same rate of interest.)
5. All actual and potential market participants have perfectly and costlessly acquired information concerning all prices and production processes, including the location and quality of all competing opportunities.

Let us now assume the existence of a labor market operating in an economy characterized by the above assumptions. We will further suppose that race discrimination exists in this hypothetical society. Discrimination, in this case, means that at the going rate of wages many businesses will exclude workers of a particular race (or gender, religion, caste, sexual preference, etc., – again, the model has been generalized to a wide variety of types of discrimination).[1]

In the event that some employers practice discrimination in hiring, its most immediate effect is that those firms are denying themselves access to a portion of the available labor pool. In the language of this analysis the reason for this discrimination is that, in the eyes of prejudiced employers, minority workers are simultaneously "producing" two items. The first is the work-effort that all (otherwise identical) workers are paid to contribute. The second is the "race quality" that discriminating employers find objectionable. (This is the source of the controversial phrase "taste for discrimination" initially advanced by University of Chicago economist Gary Becker.)

Now, suppose that there are enough persons of the privileged race to fill all positions in discriminating firms. If we further assume that all workers exclusively care about their own individual wage, then in the event of perfect competition discriminating firms will find enough workers to satisfy their perceived need for a workplace entirely constituted of the racial characteristics they prefer. Following the assumptions of perfect competition posited above, "minority" workers will be able to costlessly locate and secure jobs at the market rate of wages at other, non-discriminating, firms. The final outcome will feature no effect on anyone's wages, but there will be an effect on the distribution of employees. Some firms will have exclusively white employees, whereas non-discriminating firms will have, relative to the entire population, a disproportionate number of minority employees.

But, one might reasonably ask, what if a substantial percentage of all firms were owned by prejudiced persons? In fact, let us suppose that so many firms are owned by prejudiced persons that it is impossible for them to hire exclusively from the privileged race. Conversely, there may be too few unprejudiced employers to hire all of the discriminated-against workers. Under these conditions, some minority employees are forced to seek out positions at discriminating firms. If these workers are to "induce" discriminating firms to accept their applications for employment, they must offer to perform the same work as their privileged peers for a reduced wage. In short, they must accept a reduced wage if they are to offset the "distaste" of discriminating employers in hiring them.[2] Depending upon the intensity of discrimination felt by any given employer, they will face a larger or smaller reduction in wages. Of course it is conceivable, as a matter of logic, that this "discount" could be 100 percent. However, it is an implicit preconception of this theory that "rational discriminators" will be willing to hire minority workers for some non-zero wage. For that reason we will maintain that assumption here.

If we further assume that employer prejudice varies in intensity along a continuous scale, discriminated-against employees have an incentive to seek out the least prejudiced employer first. Drawing upon the assumption of perfect information, such a search is costless. Consequently, discriminated-against workers will initially fill positions at non-discriminating firms, then search for positions at the lesser discriminating firms, turn next to moderately discriminating firms, and so forth, until all minority workers have secured employment.

Now – and this is critical – we have assumed that all workers are perfect substitutes for one another with regard to ability, efficiency, and productivity. Since, under the assumptions of perfect competition, similar "goods" must sell at the same price, it follows that workers with identical qualities must all be paid the same wage. (This is an extension of the law of one price discussed in previous lectures.) Since discriminated-against workers are all identical to each other in every aspect, it follows that they will all, *independently of the variety of firm that actually employs them* (i.e. discriminatory or non-discriminatory), be paid the same wage. Consequently a "dual wage structure" will emerge. It will feature a "privileged" wage and a "minority" wage – with the latter set at a level that enables all minority job seekers to find employment. This conclusion is consistent with the "race premium" that was long a distinguishing characteristic of labor market discrimination (Lester 1941, 202–06, see also his several references).

Notice that for a dual wage structure to emerge, it is unnecessary that each and every employer be prejudiced. All that is required is that there be more minority employees than positions at non-prejudiced employers. The second condition is that all employers are "rational" in the sense that even non-discriminatory employers exclusively seek to maximize profits. It follows that if non-discriminating firms can hire minority employees at a discount, they can be expected to seize the opportunity.

Considered from the perspective of firms, a most interesting and profitable opportunity is presented by the existence of prejudice elsewhere in the labor market. This is because unprejudiced firms will experience an economic windfall. After all, these firms were previously willing to pay the full market wage for labor without regard to race. As profit-making non-discriminating firms, their exclusive interest is to fully staff their workplaces. However, these non-discriminating firms have found, to their undoubted delight, that they can now save on labor costs by hiring discriminated-against workers at the discounted "minority wage." This provides unprejudiced firms with more profit than they otherwise would have reason to expect. These are profits that they can use to invest and expand their market share at the expense of their competitors – discriminating firms.

Discriminating firms, on the other hand, must operate in the same product and labor markets but they also confront a unique obstacle.

To the owners or managers of these firms the discounted "minority wage" represents "compensation" for the "psychic cost" they experience from hiring and working with persons against whom they are prejudiced. The savings on wages they accrue from underpaying minority workers represents, in their view, a necessary bonus, undoubtedly taken in some form of consumption, that "compensates" them for the discomfort they have experienced. In their minds the "compensating discount" is just adequate to induce them to hire minority employees. It follows that, on average, these firms will employ a disproportionately greater number of the higher-paid privileged workers than their unprejudiced competitors. The latter, seeing only an easy opportunity for enhanced profits, will actually seek out minority workers so as to acquire as much of the labor they need at a reduced cost.

As a direct consequence of the prejudices of their owners or managers, discriminating firms must contend with higher wage costs. Moreover, the profits they will be able to accumulate for further investment will be less than that of their non-discriminating competitors. With lower rates of investment discriminating firms will be unable to expand as rapidly as their unprejudiced competitors, so their market share can be expected to decline over time. Non-discriminating firms, with higher rates of investment and growth, will come to command a larger percentage of the markets for output and labor. As the share of discriminating firms declines, and that of non-discriminating firms expands, the wage discount that minority workers must accept will also decline. Over time, the wages of all equally qualified workers will converge on a single market wage. The only remaining residue of discrimination will be that the remaining, and increasingly inconsequential, prejudiced firms will still employ labor forces made up exclusively of the privileged group.

The larger lesson of the "Chicago School" theory of discrimination is that in the presence of free market forces, the material effects of labor market discrimination can be expected to wither away. Although a few "die-hard" firms will continue to practice discrimination, and hire exclusively privileged workers, these firms will be increasingly at the margins of the larger labor market and society as a whole. Over time, their employees will be privileged exclusively in the historical sense – the wage premiums they once had will be long gone.

Another and important conclusion drawn is that the most effective way to erode the material effects of discriminatory practices is through market competition. The "weapon of choice" to a despised group is the acceptance of wage discounts. From such an argument it is inferred that government efforts to legislate "equal wages for equal work" will, perversely, maintain discriminatory practices. The argument is that such laws undermine the ability of unprejudiced firms to garner exceptional profits and thereby expand their market share. Such laws, these authors contend, enable prejudiced firms to continue their labor market practices without fear of competition from unprejudiced rivals. This is one of the reasons that Chicago School economists have long argued against minimum wage laws, maximum hours laws, "equal opportunity" laws, and other well-intentioned labor market interventions. They believe that they each and severally undermine the capacity of a "free market" to create, over time, a society of more genuinely equal opportunity (Friedman, 1962, ch. 7; Becker, 1968, 1971; Sowell, 1981a).

The processes described above will be accelerated in the event that discriminated-against workers are able to turn to profit-oriented and competitive technology and financial markets to start firms of their own. Given the conventional assumptions of perfect competition, no obstacles should obstruct the founding or expansion of firms owned by non-discriminating employers. This flurry of entrepreneurial activity will even more rapidly expand opportunities for discriminated-against employees. With more opportunities for employment, the "privileged" wage and the "minority" wage can be expected to even more quickly converge.

In the end, firms owned or managed by prejudiced persons will be confronted with a choice that is as hard as it is inescapable. They can continue to operate with the services of well-paid privileged workers while indulging their sense of prejudice. Or, they can stifle their inclination to discriminate and employ minority workers at a discount. This latter strategy enables the firm to grow and prosper. The former strategy will inevitably lead to their firm's marginalization or even elimination in a competitive market.

It is consistent with the ethos of the "free market" Chicago School that it is not the government that penalizes discriminating firms. On the contrary, "penalties" are imposed by impersonal market forces exclusively motivated by private self-interest. In a competitive market, firms refusing to hire the most qualified workers available at the lowest wage will have less profits with which to expand their enterprises. By indulging their prejudices rather than attending to "the bottom line" these firms are penalized by market forces. The Chicago School of economists is confident that the penalty to "indulging" one's "taste for discrimination" is as substantial as it is inevitable.

An extension of the above analysis is the proposition that, in the event that the discriminating firm is owned by profit-seeking shareholders, that is to say that it is a private corporation, minorities will be in an even more favorable position. The reason is that self-interested shareholders have every incentive to replace discriminating executives and managers. After all, shareholders stand to earn higher levels of profit per share if they operate their company with non-discriminating executives and managers. Even if the shareholders are themselves prejudiced, they will not be themselves obliged to work with the outcast group, and their self-interest will constrain managers who might otherwise exhibit a "taste for discrimination." Extending the Chicago School perspective, Thomas Sowell has argued that for-profit corporations are less likely to discriminate than non-profit entities such as museums or universities. For similar reasons he claims that monopolies, since they are protected from competition, also retain the ability to indulge a "taste for discrimination" over time (Sowell, 1981a, ch. 3).

Sowell's argument is along the following lines. Imagine an isolated community whose economy is dominated by a large employer. Let us further suppose that this prominent employer is organized by an equally prominent union that has negotiated for a wage higher than the "prevailing market wage." All workers not employed by this dominant firm must work for another of the town's employers. These latter firms are smaller and pay the prevailing market wage. In such a case, the owners or managers of the dominant firm may freely indulge their proclivity toward discrimination because they have the luxury of selecting from among a surplus of applicants for whatever qualities they, for whatever reasons, may prefer. This may be employees who are white, male, or straight. They may select all of the above, none of the above, or even their inverse. If enough applicants of the favored group are available to fill all the jobs at this dominant firm, the workplace will be completely segregated. Moreover, this condition may be sustainable for an extended period.[3]

The larger lesson of the above analysis is that the solution to discrimination is to eliminate any and all limitations on the scope and functioning of competitive markets (Friedman, 1962, ch. 7; Becker, 1968; Sowell, 1981a). Such a policy will operate on a fatal weakness of discrimination – it is poor business practice. The principle is that market forces are Darwinian processes that ruthlessly undermine inefficient enterprises, without care or concern for the origin of a given firm's inefficiencies. It follows that competition will weed out discriminating firms as relentlessly as it weeds out incompetent management, outdated technology, or unfashionable products.

The Chicago School economists all agree that owners and managers who require "compensation," in the form of a wage discount, to hire minority workers are certainly harming their employees. But their attention is generally focused on the longer term wherein discriminatory owners and managers succeed only in bringing harm to themselves. As they see it, the situation is analogous to those people who refuse to shop in minority-owned or staffed shops or restaurants. They will only reduce the range of choices and prices from which they can select. In their view, prejudiced shoppers should have every right to indulge their biases, but they will also, on average, pay more for less. Before too long, they maintain, the "invisible hand" will draw patronage to the cheaper shops.[4]

THE MARKET ECONOMY AND DISCRIMINATION

Can Differentials in Economic Opportunity and Remuneration Continue to Exist?

Let us now reiterate several points. First, the Chicago School theory does not prove that the market mechanism will eliminate previously-existing discriminatory practices. Rather it deduces such a conclusion by considering the implications of a particular economic theory, one that features a specific set of assumptions concerning the structure and dynamics of output and labor markets. Specifically, the theory assumes that the economic system can be plausibly represented as having highly competitive markets. From this beginning it follows that the market will eliminate the economic consequences of discrimination. All of the above leads to the following conclusion, one that is of critical importance for contemporary policy discussions. If we have a reasonably free-market economy and accept the Chicago

School theory of the economics of discrimination to be broadly accurate, then we must conclude that the remaining differentials in economic attainment must be attributed to some existing and persisting extra-market condition or constraint.

Hypothetically, suppose we were to accept the above theory. Suppose that we also accepted the proposition that labor markets have been reasonably competitive for a substantial period of time. Jointly, these require us to consider an important question. How is it that substantial differentials in employment and compensation continue to exist and even persist between any two populations (or genders, or castes, etc.)? Again, if we accept the arguments summarized in this lecture, logic dictates that the lower remuneration of any particular "minority" group *must* occur because our assumption of equally capable workers is inaccurate.

This last conclusion bears repeating since the implications are substantial. If one believes that: (1) The Chicago School theory of discrimination is accurate and (2) That differential levels of employment compensation and opportunity remain and persist across two distinct social groups, then it follows that there *must be* substantive and lasting differences between the average ability or disposition of employees between the populations one is studying.

This conclusion follows directly from the structure of the theory, as there is no other explanation for the sustained differences in compensation. If a social scientist, citizen, or politician remains concerned about this persistent inequality, and wishes to address it, the set of workable solutions is both revealed and constrained by the structure of the analysis. It must be to identify and reduce any pre-market or extra-market characteristics responsible for differences in productivity between groups. With such an end in mind, several explanations have been advanced to reconcile the existence of continuing economic inequality with the presumptive competitiveness of the American economy and the presumed veracity of the Chicago School theory of discrimination.

First, is the proposition that an "anti-market culture" or some otherwise dysfunctional "prevailing attitude" allegedly adopted by some social groups is limiting their assimilation and thereby economic achievement (Steele, 1990; D'Souza, 1995). In one of the more thoughtful books of this genre, Thomas Sowell argues that immigrant groups emerging from peasant backgrounds take longer to adjust to the norms and values of capitalist markets relative to immigrant populations more experienced with urban and marketized settings. He identifies the Irish refugees of the Great Famine and African-American refugees from the early twentieth century Jim Crow South as examples of peasant societies that have been relatively slow assimilators (Sowell, 1981b). In American political circles, this explanation has been labeled "conservative."

A second explanation ascribes gaps in earnings and economic opportunity to differentials in education. The problem, according to this explanation, is neither discrimination nor the functioning of the labor market. Rather low productivity and economic remuneration are thought to be a consequence of "failed" schools. The poor quality of the school, or the low expectations of the nation's teachers and school administrators, are to blame – not employers or the structure of markets. It follows that the solution is to leave the markets alone while improving the schools which, it is supposed from the way the problem is structured, "must be" failing minority students (Welch, 1973). In American policy circles, this explanation has been labeled "liberal."

A third explanation is one that those of us who came of age in the 1970s had thought, or perhaps more accurately had hoped, was *passé*. But one should never underestimate the power of poor ideas backed by substantial sums of money. Thanks to the "generosity" of the Bradley Foundation, economist Charles Murray and his co-author, the late Harvard psychologist Richard Herrnstein, famously argued that the explanation for the sustained gap in compensation occurs because African-Americans are inherently, that is to say biologically, less capable persons. For this reason they are less productive employees and therefore paid less than the broader population (Herrnstein and Murray, 1994). Since this book received substantial criticism when it was published, I will refrain from rehashing these arguments here. However, I will recommend a detailed and critical review of its empirical claims by the University of Wisconsin econometricians Arthur Goldberger and Charles Manski (Goldberger and Manski, 1995).[5]

Each of the above arguments has a common origin. They have been advanced to explain sustained inequality in wages, opportunity, and achievement in light of the long-standing existence of competitive markets in American society. The common theme running through these perspectives is that they all implicitly or explicitly accept the Neoclassical or Chicago School position that the labor market cannot be an independent cause or contributor to the social pathology of racism (or sexism, or discrimination by caste, religion, sexual preference, etc.).

The Chicago School theory, it should be clear by now, is distinctive for its position that the market mechanism, if given full reign, will quickly and effectively undermine unprofitable prejudices and institutions. This includes discrimination. Chicago School economists such as Milton Friedman, Gary Becker, and Thomas Sowell have persistently maintained that the more competitive the market, the stronger these ameliorative forces will be. The reason, as we have seen, is not the altruism or superior moral conduct of private employers. On the contrary, with firms seeking only their own self-interest in competitive markets, we can expect to see a relatively rapid convergence of economic opportunities across all social divisions: racial, ethnic, religious, gender, etc. As mentioned, this conclusion follows so long as the underlying productivity of minority groups is identical to that of the privileged group or groups. This theory does allow for exceptions. As discussed above all organizations insulated from market forces, including non-profit institutions and for-profit monopolies, can stave off pressures to integrate. Finally, these authors contend that government regulation of the labor market, no matter how well intentioned, will diminish the market's ability to erode discriminatory practices.

NOTES

1. I am aware that there have been analytically important differences in the form and meaning of discrimination over the course of history. For this reason I will remind the reader that this and the next lecture are not to be taken as a comprehensive treatment of discrimination. They are designed to be part of an introduction to economics, and specifically to illustrate that when conditions change in a market, the assumptions and analysis may also change. Those looking for more detailed, but readable treatments of the economics of race and discrimination should consult Andrews (1999) or Loury (1998, 2002). For a more historical treatment, see Colander et al. (2004).
2. Alternatively, they could accept harsher or more onerous workplace conditions. For example, minority workers might be crowded into undesirable shifts or asked to perform more demanding tasks. Thomas Maloney and Warren C. Whatley have found that this was the case at the Ford Motor Company (Maloney and Whatley, 1995). In the case of gender discrimination, the issues are familiar. Leaving more overt sexual demands to one side, less frightening, but nevertheless unpleasant forms of what we would now term "sexual harassment" have long typified the American workplace. For example, in the 1970s one prominent Georgia law firm

expected, "all in good fun" of course, its young women interns and associates to entertain their colleagues at the firm's annual summer retreat with a "wet-T-shirt" performance. More mundanely and conventionally, the "office culture" of a firm might pressure women workers to perform minor, but gender-reinforcing, tasks for the boss and the men of the workplace. Examples have long included making the coffee before staff or client meetings, cleaning up after such meetings, watering the plants in the office, etc. In short, jobs that no one would expect male employees to perform.

3. Historically, things rarely work this way. What appears to be desired is not segregation per se, but the recognition and affirmation of a certain hierarchy at the workplace. For example, management may be all college-educated Protestant white males. The factory floor may be dominated by white men of a different ethnic or religious background (say, Irish Catholic immigrants). The cleaning staff may be all black men, and the kitchen staffed exclusively by women, perhaps with white women in managerial positions. Gays and lesbians will conceal their identities. The point is that mixed ethnicity and gender workplaces have been common in American history, even under conditions of extreme and unabashed prejudice. The issue is more frequently over the comparative status of their jobs and how much different groups are paid.

4. Readers may have already discerned that an unargued subtext of this theory of discrimination is that short period harms have few lasting effects. As with the theory itself, this can and has been challenged.

5. For an accessible discussion and criticism of the revival of biological theories of race in our era, see Graves, 2001.

LECTURE VIII

The economics of discrimination: the "structural" approach

The Chicago School theory of discrimination has been the dominant view of the economics profession since the late 1970s. As can be discerned from the previous chapter, it has also been at the foundation of virtually all discussions of how the United States should address its legacy of labor market discrimination. This is not too surprising as market-oriented approaches to social and economic problems have been in ascendance since the late 1970s.

There has, nevertheless, been some dissent from this consensus. One point is related to the very meaning of discrimination. To review, the term means that an identifiable group of persons are, by virtue of their race, gender, religion, caste, sexual preference, or some other criteria unrelated to skill or job performance, systematically disadvantaged in some market or markets. The site of discrimination may be in the realm of production or consumption. For examples of discrimination in the sphere of consumption, consider "whites only" restaurants, real estate developments, schools, or country clubs.

Discrimination, interpreted this way, denies the validity of an important assumption underlying the model presented in the previous lecture. There, "free entry and exit" was assumed to be operative in all output markets. Initially, it might appear to be obvious that expanding the size of the market would be in the interest of all producers. But, historically, the right to enjoy the services of every hotel, restaurant, or other "public accommodation" was not a spontaneous consequence of market pressures. On the contrary, equal access to such "public accommodations" would not be firmly established until the Supreme Court upheld the 1964 Civil Rights Act in December of that same year. In short, the conventional assumption of "free entry and exit" was not simply false – it required a Supreme Court ruling to come into effect.

The previous paragraph suggests that "free entry and exit" may be neither an inherent quality nor spontaneous consequence of market processes. On the contrary, American economic, legal, and social history collectively affirms that classification and exclusion along the lines of race, gender, national origin, religion or sexual orientation can readily co-exist with free markets. History suggests that formal equality and inclusiveness typically have to be mandated and enforced by law.[1] To consider what a theory of discrimination would look like if it embodied such contrary premises, this lecture will present what I will call a "structural" theory of labor market discrimination. But it must be noted that what follows is far from the only "structural" theory of discrimination in markets. Its advantage is that it is historically important and relatively straightforward to learn. For these reasons it is most suited to a book on elementary economics.[2]

The essential "stylized fact" of the structural theory of discrimination is the proposition that for some reason – a reason that can and does vary – the labor market is segmented. This division can occur along the lines of race, gender, religion, caste, or sexual orientation. The origin of this division could follow from a variety of causes. Formal legal restrictions, widely accepted social norms, or conventional social practices and biases could each or severally be responsible. An example would be the expectations, real or perceived, of a firm's current labor force. In a racist or sexist society a person might be, or believe they might be, stigmatized or dishonored if they work with a person of the "wrong" race or gender. Customer expectations constitute another, distinct, and historically important constraint on a firm's hiring practices.

To the above considerations, let us also add the observation, one that holds across a substantial swath of the economy, that qualifications are important for entry-level positions only to the extent that firms need their new hires to meet a "competence threshold." Stated simply, most employers do not expect their new hires to know the job. What they do require are employees who show signs of being willing and able to learn and "fit in."

To illustrate the importance of these generalizations, consider Barbara Bergmann's (1974) discussion of how the staff of different qualities of restaurants come to be entirely of one or another gender. It is evident that this "gendering" of restaurants is not a matter of innate skill or ability, as table service is almost always learned "on the job." Yet for a long time it was conventionally "understood" that only men should serve customers at "upscale" restaurants. Equally widely-held was the convention that only women should serve customers at "diners" or "downscale" restaurants. Yet the skills drawn upon to perform each of these jobs are similar and it is not inherently harder to learn the particular practices of one venue over the other. No qualities mark one or the other kind of restaurant as clearly and exclusively the domain of a particular gender.[3]

Despite the clear absence of an underlying logic, when gendered hiring practices exist over a substantial period of time they became "naturalized." That is to say that they become the norm in the public mind. Once this naturalization has occurred, customers will come, at least in part, to associate the quality of their dining experience with the meeting of their expectations as to what now constitutes a "normal" or "reasonable" practice. Being more concerned for profits than social justice or equality of opportunity, firms will be loath to challenge or violate these expectations. On the contrary, it is likely that they share these norms in addition to feeling an obligation, dictated by their customers, to follow them. Of course, when firms choose to conform to these expectations, their decision further reinforces them in the public mind. Consequently the "naturalization" of the gendered hiring practice is even further advanced. Even those employers who privately disapprove of this now-widely established social norm will feel compelled, socially and economically, to respect these entrenched expectations.[4] A failure to respect widely-held social conventions means that the innovative employer will be jeopardizing their all-important "bottom line" (Bergmann, 1996, ch. 3). They also risk losing their credit-worthiness, as they are also putting their banker at risk. If the bank responds by not renewing their line of credit, the viability of the firm will certainly be threatened. To sum up, any widely-held attitude, norm, social convention, or practice can constitute the foundation of a "structural theory" of discrimination.[5]

Historians, sociologists, and psychologists tell us that discrimination is usually the consequence of a multitude of preconceptions, fears, anticipations and experiences interacting in a given situation. Issues of identity, good repute in the community, perceptions of "decency" or "modesty" each and severally interact in the formation of some activity or practice that constitutes prejudice or discrimination in hiring.

But peoples' response to discrimination is not simply passive. It is well known that members of discriminated-against groups can, upon occasion, act in a manner that may even appear to validate conventional expectations or biases. An important reason for the latter response is, of course, prudence. Another is that a socially-accepted convention or norm, even those that are generally oppressive, can be permissible in some, albeit highly circumscribed, ways. To more fully grasp these points let us illustrate the theory of structural discrimination with an example from American history.

At the beginning of the twentieth century it was considered "indecent" for a young woman to work at a bar or a saloon owned by anyone other than her father or husband. The reason was that any "unattached" women in a bar was presumed to be a prostitute. Consequently those men who were concerned with their standing in the community would avoid drinking establishments where prostitution might be taking place, and where "disreputable" individuals, men or women, might be found. This interaction of variables created, in effect, a "self-fulfilling prophesy" in which taverns that employed women would find themselves catering to "down-scale" clienteles. That is to say its patrons would be disproportionately made up of men whose reputations were not at risk if they were thought to be associating with prostitutes. The preponderance of such patrons usually discouraged women from seeking employment in such establishments, unless they were in fact prostitutes or otherwise indifferent to their social reputations. In effect, the dynamics of the marketplace reinforced a widely-held social belief. As a consequence of the interaction of strongly-held expectations and market forces, "respectable" women would avoid taverns – as employees or patrons.

The considerations described above were not the only obstacle to the employment of women in taverns. Owners of taverns that employed women were at risk of having town or city officials revoke their liquor licenses or take a disproportionate interest in penalizing relatively minor infractions, etc. Safety and the inconsistent protection of the law were also barriers to women's employment in this industry. Reflecting the widespread expectations described above, if a woman employed in a tavern were to be mistreated, she would be less likely to receive a sympathetic hearing from the police, the courts, or public opinion. The reason, of course, was that most people would be inclined to share the conventional perspective on her presumed lack of "virtue" and for that reason tend to blame her for the incident. Should they come to believe that she actually was a legitimate bartender or waitress who was the victim of an assault, they might still play down her grievance, proclaiming "Well, what did she expect?"[6]

Of course, social scientists have long understood that economic interest plays an important role in the shaping of norms and conventions. At a minimum, individuals and firms come to have a vested interest in the continuation of those norms and conventions of which they are the direct beneficiaries. Of interest here is the proposition that labor market discrimination can persist when an important group obtains, and is able to sustain, an economic advantage from it. It follows that a privileged group, one with political influence, may have a direct interest in sustaining a social practice that results in labor market segmentation – if this is to their collective benefit.

To move to a more analytical plane, consider an economy, let us call it a city, featuring two broad classifications of jobs. The first we will call the "industrial" or "primary" sector. The second will be called the "services" or "secondary" sector. Let us further assume that the skills required for an entry-level position in either sector are identical. However, once hired, "on-the-job-training" (OJT) provides the employees of each sector with unique "job-specific" skills that are not readily transferable. As a consequence, anyone wishing to change sectors in mid-career has to begin anew. This affirms that it is costly for workers to switch sectors after acquiring some seniority.

Now, let us suppose that those who work in the "industrial" sector have successfully restricted their numbers by excluding workers of some readily ascertainable quality (such as race or gender). It follows that the quantity of labor supplied to the "industrial" sector would be reduced and wages would be higher than if the city's labor market were characterized by "free entry and exit."

In Figure VIII.1 the restricted supply of labor to the "industrial" sector is illustrated by the leftward shift in the labor supply schedule (from S_{w1} to S_{w2}). Recall, once more, that these graphs are read from left to right, so that a shift to the left signals a *reduced* supply, that is to say a reduced quantity of labor supplied at each and every wage level, *ceteris paribus*.

The horizontal axis, which tracks the quantity of labor, affirms that after adjusting to the restriction, the industrial sector will employ fewer workers. The vertical axis on Figure VIII.1, which displays wage levels, affirms that the workers remaining will earn higher wages. (This should be interpreted as an "average" wage paid in this sector

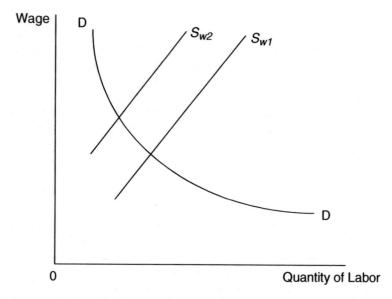

Figure VIII.1   Employment in the "Primary Sector"

since employees earn more with seniority.) These workers clearly
"win" from this arrangement. Moreover, we can expect that these
privileged workers will be interested in maintaining or even strength-
ening the conventions, norms, or social practices that restricted
competition in this "industrial" or "primary" sector.

   In the "real world," especially one that values norms such as equality and meritocracy, it is necessary to "explain" the exclusion of some
otherwise eligible workers from a given sector of the economy.
Institutional economists have labeled such explanations "enabling
myths" (Dugger, 1989). Enabling myths can take an almost infinite
variety of forms, varying as widely as the human imagination. But
some of them have become familiar through their frequent appearance across many cultures and societies. These include the following
claims: "African-Americans are not smart enough for industrial
work," or "Women are too delicate for factory jobs," or "The Chinese
are culturally predisposed to work for inhumanely low wages."

   Historically, when people have an economic interest in a belief
that defies logic or widely-available experience, enabling myths are
recast and defended as ethical imperatives. To see the power of
such rhetoric, consider the three statements that closed the previous

paragraph after they are rephrased as moral imperatives: "God did not intend for blacks and whites to work side-by-side." "The morality of the nation's children will be compromised if women work in a factory." "God intended California to be settled and civilized by white men." I am confident that every reader can readily conjure up a number of past (and current) enabling myths, and reformulate them as ethical imperatives.

The value of labor market segregation to a privileged group depends on their numbers relative to the excluded group. Additionally, it depends on how much it would cost employers to deploy labor-saving devices and/or raise the price of the goods being produced. Bergmann points out that the value of the "white employment premium" was, as a consequence of the above considerations, much higher in apartheid South Africa than in the United States of the post-war era. The reason was that in South Africa the excluded group was substantially larger than the included group. In the United States, white labor has been in the majority. However, this generalization has not been true for all eras and all regions. For example, the wage premium for white employees was higher in the post Civil War southern states before the Great Migration of black labor to the north in the early twentieth century. Wage premiums existed in the northern states too, as Irish and Eastern European immigrants were initially viewed as "races" that were altogether different from persons of English and German heritage, and for that reason subject to discrimination.

In the structural theory of occupational segregation, some identifiable subset of workers are, through one pretext or another, excluded from jobs in the primary labor market. From this it follows that the supply of labor to the "secondary" labor market – what is here termed the "services" sector – is increased. Graphically, the supply of labor function in the "services" sector shifts to the right. This reflects a greater supply of labor available to this sector at each and every wage rate. An additional consequence is that the average wage in the secondary sector is reduced.

These considerations are illustrated in Figure VIII.2, which depicts the "secondary" labor market. Reflecting the existence of what economists have termed "occupational crowding," the labor supply schedule has been shifted from S_{w3} to S_{w4}. This is solely a consequence of labor market discrimination, and workers in this market earn a reduced wage despite our assumption that workers of all races (or genders, etc.) are equally capable and motivated. Likewise, the

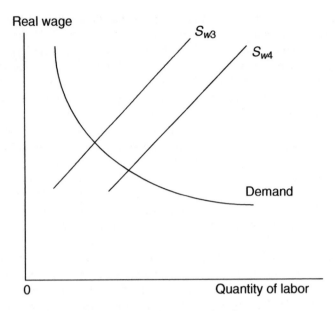

Figure VIII.2   Employment in the "secondary" sector

average wage in the industrial or "primary" sector is, and will remain, higher than average wages in the secondary or "services" sector. This wage gap is, to reiterate, unrelated to the abilities, skills, education, or motivation of the workers employed in each sector.

From the above, it is evident that the labor force of the services sector is made up of two groups: (1) Members of the privileged group not fortunate enough to obtain employment in the primary sector, and (2) All discriminated-against workers.[7] It is evident that the supply of labor to this sector is larger, and wages are lower, than if discriminatory hiring practices did not occur. We will return to this crucial point.

An important inference we can draw from a "societal" point of view, that is to say from the perspective of maximum output, is that labor is being allocated inefficiently. In the presence of discrimination it is evident that there is underproduction in the industrial sector while there is overproduction in the services sector. The size of this imbalance of productive effort depends upon a variety of conditions beyond the scope of an introductory book. But, independently of the size and value of this misdirection of productive effort, the conclusion remains that occupational segregation is socially dysfunctional.[8]

Although, considered as a whole, society is worse off in the presence of labor market discrimination, it would be incorrect to infer that everyone loses. On the contrary, two subgroups are clear beneficiaries. The first beneficiaries are primary sector employees. They receive a higher average wage as a direct result of reduced competition in their segment of the labor market. Secondary sector employers also benefit since they have access to a greater quantity of workers. Having a greater supply of labor while paying a reduced average wage enables them to produce for a larger market.[9] As beneficiaries of discriminatory hiring practices, we should expect primary sector employees and secondary market employers to be supporters of the norms, social practices, and enabling myths that underlie and validate what is to them a most satisfactory outcome.

Of most interest, from the perspective of things potentially changing, are the attitudes and outlooks of primary market employers and secondary market employees. Discrimination in the primary labor market clearly disadvantages these two subgroups. If they could or would find a way to negotiate and contract they could each benefit. Access to a greater quantity of labor would allow primary sector firms to reduce the rate of wages they must pay while increasing their output. Secondary market employees would also benefit from higher wages. Notice also that even those secondary market employees who do not change jobs would experience wage gains with the end of discrimination in hiring. The reason is that wages would rise across the entire secondary sector as the overall supply of labor in that sector is reduced.

By contracting with each other each of these two groups will be able to undercut the privileged positions and artificially high remuneration of their rivals: primary sector employees and secondary market employers. The economic benefits to each aggrieved group are clear. In a world of perfect competition and no social, political, or economic obstacles, such contracting can be expected to occur. If we do not see such contracting taking place, it is plausible that some structure or structures must be preventing it (hence the Structural Theory of Discrimination).

If the discrimination represented in Figures VIII.1 and VIII.2 is to be sustained, some reason, necessarily social and historical in nature, is required to explain why people are not making otherwise mutually-advantageous exchanges. This reason may not be simple or obvious and the reader should know that many economists, especially those influenced by the Chicago School, do not believe that such conditions can exist for long if mutually-advantageous trades can be made. That said, let us enumerate a few possibilities, even as we acknowledge that every situation of discrimination is unique and has its own particularities in addition to enabling myths to support it.

One possibility is that primary market employers might forgo hiring workers out of the secondary labor market if they believed that the losses they incurred by paying premium wages were small relative to the direct and indirect costs of challenging a widespread norm of discrimination. This would be plausible if they were confronted with a well-organized primary-sector craft union with a proven ability to strike. Another obstacle could be strongly entrenched prejudices on the part of the firm's customers or suppliers. In such cases the cost of challenging entrenched labor market practices could be high relative to the savings that would accrue from lower wage costs.

Under such conditions, even unprejudiced but profit-maximizing employers might be reluctant to hire secondary market workers. Finding no employers to contract with, secondary market workers would have to remain in their current positions. This would be true independently of any desire on their part to improve their individual or collective situation. It takes two parties to achieve a contract and primary sector employers have decided that the costs of challenging the *status quo* are not worth it.

We can complete our story by taking a closer look at the situation of secondary market workers. Are they "rational economic agents" freely seeking the highest wage, or can we suppose that they also face barriers to independent action? Drawing upon history, we find a multitude of instances wherein the losses experienced by workers crowded into secondary labor markets fail to be registered as "legitimate" economic or political grievances. This occurs when such workers are politically disenfranchised and thereby subject to random acts of violence. In such cases, it could be personally hazardous to seek to improve one's economic condition as one might find that both the larger community and its system of "justice" are unwilling to validate or protect such an action. Another contributing factor is learned passivity. Economists tend to eschew social psychological arguments, but we know of many historical situations in which oppressed people come to accept their situation as "natural," "normal," or "consistent with God's Will."[10] Even if a discriminated-against population is willing to resist, there is generally a coordination problem in that those who make the first move, or make the initial effort to organize the others, will be treated harshly. Keeping people divided to facilitate control over them is one of the most ancient arts deployed by the few to rule the many.

As mentioned above, historically we have found that discrimination is usually enforced and sustained by a combination of the above causes. Primary market employers who are unwilling or unable to undertake the costs of challenging entrenched norms co-exist with secondary market workers subdued by a combination of legal restrictions and widespread social practices and enabling myths acting in conjunction with learned passivity. It is important to note that the law, in almost every instance, tends to side with society's most powerful economic interests, which in this example includes privileged workers and secondary sector employers.

Under the conditions summarized in the previous paragraph, it is evident that secondary market employees challenging discriminatory practices are taking substantial risks for highly uncertain rewards. Not surprisingly, we find that their efforts to disrupt the existing labor market structure are often thwarted by the political and economic strength of those interested in maintaining the *status quo*. Consequently we frequently see an "equilibrium" of sorts, in which discriminatory practices persist over an extended period.

A prominent example was the long-standing "gentleman's agreement" that, for six decades, prohibited African-Americans from playing in baseball's major leagues. It was not always this way. This prohibition, beginning in the 1880s, lasted until Jackie Robinson took the field for the Brooklyn Dodgers in 1947.[11] Such a long-standing prohibition, maintained without the assistance of the law or even a formal contract, represents a challenge to the Chicago School theory of discrimination. Here was an instance where a clear incentive existed for low payroll teams to purchase first-rate talent for second-rate wages. Moreover, information was not a problem here, as the talent of the excluded players was well understood. Because of the informal between-season "barnstorming" games in which blacks and whites played against one another, it was long understood that many of the excluded African-American baseball players would have excelled in the major leagues.

If we assume that playing talent is equally distributed across each race, then it is evident that the most highly talented white players had little if anything to lose from integration (economically speaking, that is). More at risk were the average and below-average white players. The latter would almost certainly lose their jobs to superior African-American players. Even those average white players able to keep their positions would have less bargaining power over wages. If, for the sake of the argument, we assume that one-third of players are of superior talent, one-third are average and one-third of inferior talent, then 2/3 of white players had a clear economic incentive to resist integrating the major leagues.

In keeping with the contours of the structural model posited above, owners of the Negro League teams had, along with the average and below-average white players, an economic interest in maintaining segregation. African-American players, especially those of superior ability, had an interest in moving to the better paying, to say nothing of more visible, positions in Major League Baseball. In keeping with the above theory there were clear reasons why a less-wealthy major league team would wish to contract with a highly-talented African-American baseball player. Yet the owners of the major league teams were able to maintain their "gentleman's agreement." From what historians have been able to learn about this restriction and its longevity, its persistence can be attributed to three causes: first was a concern for the prejudices of fans; second was the latent racism of most owners and managers; third was the pressure exerted on lower-payroll owners by the league and their fellow owners.

Eventually one team, the Brooklyn Dodgers, broke the agreement. Its decision was motivated by the frustration of competing with its more well-heeled rivals, the then-New York Giants and New York Yankees, to sign young talent. A second cause was the thaw in social norms concerning racism that emerged after World War II. Third, was the singular presence of a highly motivated and unprejudiced evangelical-Christian manager (Branch Rickey) who had long wished to repeal the "gentleman's agreement." Fourth, was Rickey's ability to find a highly-talented baseball player willing to enter into and live by a secret agreement not to retaliate against any and all taunts or aggression – no matter how egregious – for a period of several years. Even with such a concurrence of singular circumstances, several more decades would pass before the major leagues were fully integrated.[12]

Now, on its own, the structural theory of discrimination does not and cannot fully explain the source of the initial discrimination or the reasons for its persistence. But this flaw is not as fatal as some economists believe. In the case of race and discrimination the initial cause may not be sufficient on its own, and for this reason it is reasonable to invoke extra-market and extra-theoretical factors for a complete explanation. It follows that the structural model of discrimination, or what in the professional economics literature is sometimes called the "occupational crowding model," can be useful when we examine instances in which labor markets have been restricted by either a widespread social practice, as in the nineteenth and early twentieth century South, through explicit bargaining agreements as periodically happened with some northern craft unions and in major league baseball, or through some government edict, as with the passage of explicit Jim Crow laws across much of the South (Litwack, 1998).

NOTES

1. Heart of Atlanta Motel v. United States 379 U.S. 241 (hotel accommodations); Katzenbach v. McClung 379 U.S. 294 (patronage of restaurants); Diaz v. Pan American World Airways, Inc. 442, F. 2nd 385 (5th Cir. 1971) (male cabin attendants).
2. Structural theories are a large and heterogeneous category. Early contributions include Anne Krueger (1963), Lester Thurow (1969), and Barbara Bergmann (1974). A similar theory can be deployed to illustrate structural discrimination in consumption markets.
3. While he did not write on this specific subject, Veblen did observe that being served by men, especially in the performance of largely servile and deferential tasks, is particularly gratifying to those who wish to enhance the experience (and cost) of personal service with "conspicuous leisure." Clearly (low wage) women working efficiently to provide the best dinner at the lowest price eliminates the conspicuous leisure component of the meal and thereby the subjective value of the experience to those for whom such performances are vital (Veblen, 1899, ch. 3).
4. Such a generalization would seem to apply to some of the employees of Ollie's Barbecue, who were themselves African-American.
5. Of course, an important difference remains between a "distinction" and a "discrimination." The former represents an instance where one kind of person is differentiated from another for a reason germane to the process or activity at hand. For example, selecting the best performers to staff an orchestra is, or should be, a procedure designed to make a distinction. Discrimination occurs when an difference that is arbitrary with regard to the task at hand is the basis of selection.
6. I trust that it is clear that none of the attitudes being described here are those of the author, but that this paragraph is simply a summary of attitudes that were widely-held from the nation's founding until rather recently.
7. It would be relatively easy to extend this theory in a manner that would reflect even more "realism." Suppose that to "merit" a position in the primary labor market one had to undergo some expensive and/or onerous activity – such as additional schooling, the purchase of a suit, etc. Assuming, again, homogeneous

workers, it is plausible that all eligible workers would be willing to undertake this expense in the hope of being selected for the primary labor market. Those discriminated against, understanding that they are highly unlikely to be granted access to this market, will "rationally" decide to not make these investments. *Ex post*, primary sector employees, their employers, and the politicians who represent them, will attribute the reduced circumstances of discriminated-against workers on their "unwillingness" to make appropriate investments in schooling, attire, or other forms of public deportment. The end result is, in either case, occupational segregation. What has changed is that all workers, who were initially of homogeneous quality, would now appear to be heterogeneous. The political and social importance of this outcome cannot be overemphasized.

8. The growth rate of the post-bellum South, with its extreme racism and segregation, was significantly less than that of the northern states. Southern growth rates rose as the lawlessness of Jim Crow broke down. The relationship between these events is too complex for a footnote, but it is evident that there was an important relationship (Ransom and Sutch, 1977).

9. To be perfectly accurate, under the standard assumptions of perfect competition, "economic profits" for firms in the secondary sector will still be zero even if they operate on a larger scale than firms in the primary sector. Nevertheless, these firms still retain a stake in the status quo because eliminating the barriers preventing the movement of labor into the primary sector will force them to pay higher wages. They will then experience negative rates of economic profit until enough firms exit the market and the equilibrium condition of zero economic profit is restored. In short, firms in the secondary market have a collective interest in avoiding the costs associated with the transition to a free and fair labor market.

10. Consider the experience of women workers over the centuries. It was long thought to be "normal" or "natural" for women to not have waged positions in the workforce, especially after marriage. It was also thought to be "unfeminine" for a woman, especially a young women, to drive a hard bargain with her boss, or forcefully demand change. For women to progress in economic status and opportunity, such deeply entrenched ideologies had to be challenged at the same time that employment barriers were being challenged. While on this subject I wish to note that while the acceptance or rationalization of one's situation might be a poor long-term political strategy, it should be recognized that it has the clear merit of presenting the oppressed with short-term psychological comfort. The value of such comfort is often underestimated by economic and political theorists who have a tendency, as a result of their chosen occupation, to overemphasize the place of "economic interest" in explaining the behavior of individuals and groups. As a professional economist, I include myself as one who is prone to this error.

11. Actually, his first major league season was with Brooklyn's AAA team, the Montreal Royals in the 1946, where management thought, correctly, that he would be more readily accepted by fans. But, in keeping with the long-standing American convention that all things Canadian should be ignored, I will overlook this fact.

12. In one of the better books on the subject of baseball, David Halberstam credits the rise of the completely integrated St. Louis Cardinals team of the 1960s, led by their legendary pitcher, Bill Gibson, with establishing for once and all the idea that to win in the modern era a team had to recruit and integrate African-American players (Halberstam, 1994).

Values and prices: reintroducing ethical considerations into economics

INTRODUCTION

Non-economists often perceive economists to be immoral or, at a minimum, amoral. Periodically, this view receives strong affirmation. An example that captured the public's attention occurred in the early 1990s when Lawrence Summers, then the World Bank's Chief Economist, set off a controversy with his famous memorandum that concluded that "the economic logic behind dumping a load of toxic waste in the lowest-wage country is impeccable and we should face up to that" (*New York Times*, Feb. 7, 1992, p. D2; *Washington Post*, February 10, 1992, p. A9). Non-economists, not surprisingly, took this statement to be another sign of the profession's moral bankruptcy. Characteristically, Summers attributed the resulting controversy to "political correctness." While I will not review the specifics of this controversy, I do believe that substantial insight may be gained if we understand that Summers was simply drawing out an inference from mainstream economic theory.

Underlying the "clash of cultures" between many economists and the rest of the citizenry is a way of thinking about choices and policy that periodically reveals that the former are often prone to confuse values with prices. For example one can simply, and correctly, refute Summers' memo by observing that in our post-aristocratic era most thinking people believe that each life should be accorded an infinite value. Since this idea is unworkable in practice, ethical reasoning ascribes a high and equal value to each life. It follows that systematically imposing the disease and early demise associated with certain production processes on a select group of persons, specifically chosen because they are poor, is thought to be immoral.

Indeed, when one examines the structure of economic theory – especially in its policy-making guise wherein statements concerning "efficiency," "welfare-maximization," and "cost-benefit calculation" are reified as neutral and transcendent standards of judgment – some disturbing value judgments and premises are, in fact, unveiled. This is the case because every policy decision taken, or not taken, impacts some third party. Often this fundamental quality of decision-making is dodged or repressed by positing the existence of a depoliticized and thereby unproblematic "social welfare function." Once such a social welfare function is posited, the distribution of the several costs and benefits from a course of action, if addressed at all, are hidden behind criteria such as "the market outcome" or, worse-yet, a hypothetical standard of non-reimbursement called "Hicks–Kaldor Compensation."[1]

In sum, too many of the economists of our era are prone to reproduce Summers' error – even if they, or the institutions they work for, have become more sensitive to the consequences of letting memos such as his leak into the public realm. In short, the public pronouncements of economists, and too many applications and examples from our textbooks, suggest that a confusion between values and prices runs deep, even to the core of the economics discipline. This is important to all of us as the economics profession has been engaged in a century-long quest to establish itself as the field that presents unbiased advice on matters of public policy (Bernstein, 2001).

ON PRICES

Reduced to its simplest form, a price is the ratio at which things exchange for one another. Consider the theory of price now dominant in American economics (the theory of commodity prices described earlier). Its assumptions of perfect competition – full and free information, many competing buyers and sellers, free entry and exit, and homogeneous products – collectively imply costless arbitrage across the market. Drawing upon this theory, it is often inferred that the market price prevailing at any given time represents the summation of individual choices made by the numerous independent individual decision-makers that collectively make up the "marketplace."[2]

If we assume that we are dealing with a moment in time and thereby ignore discounting the future (nothing important changes in the analysis if we do this), many economists will confidently state that the demand curve that exists in the market is derived from the prior endowments and the (stable) preferences (drawn as "utility functions") that describe the collection of individuals trading in a particular market during a particular trading period (Becker and Stigler, 1977).[3] The market, then, is presented to readers as the realm of "choice," since the final pattern of demand can be said to reflect a summation of the choices being exercised by the multitude of persons currently trading in the market.[4] Under the conditions specified above, the market is said to be an efficient allocator of goods and services as it is thought to accurately reflect the willingness of people, given their prior preferences and endowments, to pay for a particular distribution.

When we review the above depiction of the market process, what stands out is that what is described is less a "choice" than a "calculation." This follows directly from the assumptions deployed to construct the idea of a "rational economic agent." They are, to review, highly knowledgeable; have a clear and independent understanding of their own preferences; and can draw upon sophisticated mathematics to solve for an "optimal" decision.

To explore the ethical aspects of this understanding of choice, consider the following thought experiment. Suppose we have a "rational" person whose characteristics fits standard criteria including the Walrasian principle of gross substitution. (This principle guarantees that there is a price, above zero but below infinity, at which all goods can be priced in terms of one another, thereby ensuring that the system is coherent with an equilibrium solution.) Now, let us assume a simple world of two commodities. The first is a medicine that I must have in a certain discrete, ie. non-infinitesimal, quantity to keep my sister alive. I will call this "sister's medicine." The second commodity is beer. In light of my income and the market price of each good, I can afford certain "bundles" of each of these two goods.

Now, let us suppose an optimizing agent who really loves his or her sister. This person would have a relatively flat but, being "rational," downwardly sloped utility function between sister's medicine and beer. Yet the principle of gross substitution implies that there must exist a price for beer at which our rational consumer will not purchase an adequate quantity of medicine to keep his sister alive.

According to mainstream economics, the above outcome must be both rational and efficient. However, virtually everyone else would say that such a choice is irrational – even criminal. The absurdity built into the example is that it places on a single scale two "goods" that, for most people, exist on different planes or spheres of importance or priority. Philosophers say that such goods or choices are an instance of incommensurability (Chang, 1997). One of the goods, beer, is for most of us a moderate intoxicant used exclusively for recreational purposes. The second, sister's medicine, is about the life and death of a loved one. Most sane people consider the life of their sister to be a priority over the momentary pleasure of drinking beer, and for this reason would take the above to represent a "false choice." This is exactly my point – it is a false choice.

The above example suggests that if the conventional "theory of choice" is to make sense, it must be restricted to considering the more banal decisions of life. In other words, a choice between corn or peas for dinner, or buying a navy blue or tweed jacket to wear to an economics conference, are the sort of choices best suited to consideration within this framework. The reason is that nothing fundamental is at stake so a model of choice suggesting parameters such as "preferences," "relative prices," and "budget constraints" is plausible. If peas and a navy blue jacket are relatively expensive, I will purchase corn and a tweed jacket.

No one is surprised, or should be surprised, to find that a model designed to explain the banal choices of life is lacking when something more fundamental is at stake. The limitations of this approach will become evident in two broad classes of choice discussed below. The first I will label "moral choices," the second I will label "identity choices."

MORAL CHOICES – VALUES

Moral choices, what the philosopher Martha Nussbaum calls "tragic choices," are qualitatively different from the calculations that are the ideal subject of the Neoclassical theory of choice (Nussbaum, 2001). In the latter a significant tension is present that forces the person choosing to assess or reassess their values. The reason is that the decision they are making may be laden with ethical implications.

Nussbaum believes that literature is a realm well suited to exploring tragic choices. I will follow her lead. Consider the novel *Sophie's Choice*, which poignantly captures the idea of a moral choice (Styron,

1979). In William Styron's novel, a Nazi prison camp doctor forces a young mother to choose which of her two children is to be led away to die. It trivializes the situation to describe her "choice" as a calculation in the sense that one decides to have peas or corn for dinner. Rather, she was confronted with an irresolvable moral dilemma. Sophie, the heroine of the book, after being forced to make such a choice, is tormented for the rest of her sad and shortened life.

Recently, McDonalds Corporation learned that a failure to appreciate the ethical implications that others ascribe to certain choices can result in actionable consequences. McDonalds had to admit that for years, and without informing their customers, they had used animal products to flavor their French fries. Evidently, McDonalds' management believed that those who wished to be vegetarian were free to exercise such a choice, but that such a choice was trivial. That is to say that in McDonald's view it was based upon a calculation that management could undermine without repercussions of importance for anyone concerned. What they did not, or would not, understand is that for some persons, such as practicing Hindus, vegetarianism is a moral choice and not a "preference" or "lifestyle." For that reason McDonalds' knowing misrepresentation of the qualities of one of its leading products was deeply offensive to many customers.

Without considering their ultimate foundation, the importance of moral choices for economics can be readily understood. The distinguishing feature of a moral choice is that it should not depend on price considerations. For example, the Biblical injunction "Thou shalt not kill" is not modified by the qualification that one should feel free to kill if it pays enough. While each of us may continue to disagree over the motivations and conditions under which one might nevertheless kill another person – judicially-mandated punishment, self-defense, defense of one's family or nation, under no circumstances, etc. – I am confident that all religious and philosophical frameworks concur that killing for money is wrong. It is illustrative that the level of remuneration does not constitute an extenuating consideration.

Hollywood tapped into such issues with the movie *An Indecent Proposal* (1993). Here a young wife (Demi Moore), with the consent of her husband (Woody Harrelson), agrees to spend a night with a wealthy stranger (Robert Redford), in exchange for a million dollars. The young couple initially perceives the transaction to be a pragmatic exchange that could never undermine their strong relationship. But they were wrong. For the audience, the interest and dramatic tension of the movie turned on the fact that incommensurable "goods" were being exchanged.

IDENTITY CHOICES

Somewhere between the set of neoclassical choices (calculations) and moral choices (duties, obligations) exists a third set of choices that are neither moral choices nor simple calculations. I will term this category "identity choices." To motivate this set of choices, consider the fact that anthropologists, sociologists, and marketing professionals do not think of consumption choices as taking place in a series of discrete settings by individuals who are existentially alone (ie. according to the rules of what is called "methodological individualism"). Rather, most of the non-economic literature understands that consumption plays a role in shaping a person's sense of themselves and their place in those complex spaces that we call "society." In short, consumption serves to simultaneously identify and distinguish a particular person with and from their fellows (Goffman, 1959; Lutz and Lux, 1979, chs. 1–3; Levine, 1988, ch. 1; Douglas, 1992).

These identity choices, which often appear to be arbitrary when viewed from a distance, effectively circumscribe the everyday consumption decisions of most people. That is to say their choices are not based upon an accidental configuration of preferences, relative prices, and budget constraints. Yet it would be equally incorrect to think of identity choices as moral choices, although this generalization has exceptions or at least a "gray" area. Depending on the specifics of a given culture or situation, a person's choice of food and clothing can come close to representing a moral choice. For example, during the German occupation of France in the 1940s, patriotic women wore long and flowing skirts to signal their non-compliance with the German and Vichy governments' request to spare cloth in support of the war effort.

In general, a person's choice of clothing or food is a decision that they, and their peers, feel strongly about even in the absence of a clear moral basis. In short, there is a reason, beyond a calculation based on preferences and relative prices, that I did not present this lecture to my classes while wearing a swimsuit and sunglasses. While it would not have been illegal or immoral to have done so, my choice was nevertheless constrained by the social meanings that would be implicit in such a mode of deportment. The point is that identity choices are fraught with meaning when considered in light of the interest that people have, consciously or unconsciously, in a particular self-image or sense of themselves. Within our own society certain clothing choices are identified with certain professions and contexts. What I would wish to wear to the beach is different from what I would wear in my classroom or to a job interview, and vice versa, all other things being equal.

The larger lesson is that in a complex social structure, the ability to act or, more importantly, to interact with our fellows, to efficiently complete transactions or work-related tasks, and to have satisfactory interpersonal relationships, requires a more nuanced pattern of consumption than what might be deemed necessary or convenient for biological subsistence (Prasch, 2003). When our sense of identity and social standing are involved, consumption is less about wants, or even needs, than our ability to act as members of society. As Amartya Sen put it, "The focus has to be, in this analysis, on the freedoms generated by commodities, rather than on the commodities seen on their own" (Sen, 1999, p. 74). With this more complete understanding of the dynamics of choice, we are ready to return to the previously-posited distinction between values and prices.

VALUES AND PRICES

Prices, as previously noted, are an economic category. They are the ratios at which objects trade for one another. Values, on the other hand, are grounded in considerations of ethics, religion or identity. The reason that we do not kill each other for money, or spend money on beer rather then on our sister's medicine, is not because the "price signals" from the market fail to consistently support these choices. On the contrary, we all know that for some people, today's prices are already sufficient to support perverse, dangerous, or even pathological choices. To discourage such choices we do not rely upon the price system, but impose sanctions, sometimes criminal and at other times social, to reinforce our collective disapproval. Tellingly, we often act as though at least some of our choices are larger than ourselves and our own gratification. And they are. To this end we pursue consumption patterns or agendas that identity, taboos, religion, morality or reason dictate to be ends in themselves and are, for that reason, not to be surrendered for financial considerations.

Now, as a matter of experience, we know that some people can be bought (how cheaply can be a disturbing surprise). In the case of an identity choice, "buying" someone is often, and ought to be, easier than in the case of a moral choice. For example, we have "reality" television shows that reward people for violating certain norms associated with identity, such as our resistance to eating exotic bugs. So far we seem to be spared shows in which moral choices are violated for money prizes, although *Temptation Island* comes close.[5]

Keeping the above distinctions in mind can be of assistance when we examine the arguments of economists who wish to expand the logic of markets into every investigation of social life. What they fail to understand or appreciate are the distinctions at the core of the moral systems that philosophers, theologians, and most thinking people uphold. This explains why it is that when economists argue that Christmas gifts are inefficient, or that the adoption of children could be more efficiently conducted through the market, they are thought to be missing the point, if not being amoral or even immoral.

A failure to distinguish values from prices can become distressing when economists participate in debates over social policy. When assessing the value of a clean environment or the proper level of a legislated minimum wage, most people place significant weight on moral considerations. When economists insist that these questions should be exclusively decided upon the criteria of cost–benefit analysis they are, not too surprisingly, discouraged to see that they have lost their audience.

It is now evident that George Stigler was in error when he observed that the public's support of the minimum wage demonstrated that the mass of people are ignorant of the insights that economists can contribute (Stigler, 1982, p. 57). It is unnecessary to share Stigler's perspective on the economics of the minimum wage to grasp the reason why his perspective has been rejected – to most Americans he simply failed to address the point. When considering a legislated minimum wage, most people wish to uphold a long-standing social and even religious norm that maintains that a person of able mind and body who "plays by the rules" should be able to live by their labor. As with many strongly-held values, this norm has come to be embodied in law. In other words, most Americans take the minimum wage to be an ethical, rather than an economic, issue. When the issue is examined from the perspective of values, the econometricians' analysis of that policy's effect on the employment prospects of teenagers is, independently of the results, besides the point (Waltman, 2000).

CONCLUSION

Most of us have heard the quip that "An economist is someone who knows the price of everything and the value of nothing." This joke is amusing because it embodies an element of truth. Having a developed theory of price, and a method for estimating and contrasting probable outcomes, economists have come to invest the results that follow from such analyses with more importance than they merit.

Recently, Amartya Sen summed up the essential problem, "Since the preference for market-price-based evaluation is quite strong among many economists, it is also important to point out that all variables other than commodity holdings (important matters such as mortality, morbidity, education, liberties and recognized rights) get – implicitly – a zero direct weight in evaluations based exclusively on the real-income approach" (Sen, 1999, p. 80). At times this bias has left economists on the periphery of public discussions of social, and sometimes even economic, policy. It will continue to do so until economists come to appreciate the meaning of incommensurability and what it implies for their theory of choice.

NOTES

1. When policy researchers ask themselves if, hypothetically, those who gain from a proposed policy would be able, in principle, to compensate the losers from such a policy, then the policy is said to have passed the "Hicks–Kaldor Compensation" test. Notice that this test includes no plan or proposal to actually make such compensation occur; it only demands that the gains be adequate to do so *in principle*.
2. Of course several other coherent, viable, and applicable theories of price exist, but since they are no longer part of the training or knowledge base of American economists their implications for the subject of this lecture will not be considered. For a survey of some of these other theories see Arestis (1992, ch. 6) or Lavoie (1992, ch. 3).
3. The reception accorded this paper by Becker and Stigler will someday be the basis of a fascinating history. Essentially, it announced a set of "rules" for theoretical work – rules that were neither plausible nor adequately defended – that in turn became a parameter of research and hallmark of professional conduct for a generation of economists. For a critique, along with the sketch of a viable alternative, see a recent paper by Geoffrey Hodgson (Hodgson, 2003).

4. Again, by staying within the spirit of "mainstream" analysis, I am brushing over a host of serious, and inadequately resolved, conceptual and technical problems in the actual theory itself. Those that most stand out are the aggregation problems involved in summing across a collection of individual demand curves of several individually rational actors to arrive at an aggregate demand curve. John Hicks (1939, note to ch. 9), Oscar Morgenstern (1940) and Harvey Leibenstein (1950) each present interesting analyses of the pitfalls that await the careful theorist in the process of aggregation, although they drew different conclusions as to how fatal these problems were for the theory. Finally, it must be acknowledged that theorists working within the Austrian tradition also reject this "mainstream" approach. To Ludwig Lachmann or Friedrich von Hayek and, depending on the text in question, Ludwig von Mises or Israel Kirzner, the economy is about change and adjustment to change from continually evolving states of the world, including changes in information and preferences. Taking the market to be a "process," they generally reject attempts to aggregate the demand of several individuals and are suspicious of conclusions drawn from such exercises.
5. Of course, the reason may be that moral choices are often codified into law. Either way, we do not see cannibalism or incest encouraged on "reality" shows. Or did I speak too soon?

CONCLUSION

Some reflections on economic policy

Collectively these lectures suggest that the theory of "Supply and Demand" is not as generalizable as many economists have come to suppose. A parallel concern is how effectively a market system may serve our social and individual need to reliably and reasonably allocate commodities, jobs, and assets. To a degree, this is a larger question, connected to the theory of macroeconomics, and for that reason a full answer is beyond the scope of a set of introductory lectures. But enough has been written to advance a few ideas. Here I will briefly summarize four instances where regulation, if appropriately drawn, can enhance the performance of markets.

First, well-crafted regulations can enhance the quality and quantity of information available to the customer. By this means, many "experience" goods can be transformed into "inspection" goods. (To review, experience goods are those about which one learns of their underlying qualities with the passage of time. By contrast, most of the germane qualities of inspection goods can be assessed at the time of purchase.) While such regulations may be unimportant when considering the purchase of a trinket, the situation is more serious if fraud or public health are potential considerations.

The implications of this idea are more sweeping than one might at first suppose. As James K. Galbraith argues in a recent and important paper, when people purchase a good they are actually purchasing both the item and some assurance that the product is safe and effective. For this reason "an industrial market system requires that a flow of detailed and credible information be provided about the products on offer" (Galbraith, 2007, p. 17). For a modern economy, with its inherently complex products and processes to work:

> the necessary and sufficient condition is a *credible* guarantee of product authenticity and quality. The customer must have reason to believe that

the product is what it claims to be, and that it will function as it is supposed to do. This is what a strong system of regulation provides. (Galbraith, 2007, p. 13)

Consider the following, fairly important, decision – one confronted by millions of Americans each year. What do we really know about the maintenance practices of the airline whose airplane we are about to board? To be properly informed each of us would have to acquire substantial expertise in modern aircraft and the qualities that make them operate safely. Additionally, we would have to study the business practices, procedures, and trade secrets of the several competing airlines – are they cutting back too far on their repair budgets? Is management careful with weight limits on takeoffs? Does the maintenance supervisor or the pilot have a drinking problem? The fact is that most of us know next to nothing about these questions. With no substantial basis upon which to make informed decisions concerning safety, flying on an airplane is a classic "experience" good. Left to a perfectly free market, fewer of us would choose to fly.

The solution to this problem, devised long ago, is to develop a credible program of government inspection combined with the penalizing of firms with inadequate safety records. Broadly speaking, the safety record of airlines within the United States suggests that this system has been effective. (Such regulations could, of course, be extended to prohibit the imprisonment of passengers on runways for extended periods of time – but I digress.) Believing that all airlines are reasonably well-regulated I, as the buyer of a ticket, am able to focus on variables that I understand. These include relative prices and the convenience of schedules. In such an instance, then, regulation can transform an experience good with speculative attributes into something more akin to an inspection good. Being so empowered, consumers are more likely to enter the market, which enhances demand for the product in question. Consumers and producers both emerge as "winners."

The logic sketched above finds confirmation in the historical record. In a fascinating and detailed series of essays on the early history of regulation, Marc Law shows how regulation has been deployed by business firms and professions, particularly those using new processes or technologies, as an instrument to expand markets through the creation of credible commitments to quality and safety (Law, 2003; Law and Kim, 2005). To sum up, when regulation transforms an experience good into something approaching an inspection good, it modifies the structure of the market, with the effect of increasing both its size and efficiency. Consumers and the more efficient and innovative businesses are both winners (Galbraith, 2007).

A second concern is that social costs must be accounted for and allocated. Regrettably, too many economists implicitly assume that everyone has the ability to exist or at least subsist outside of the market. Whatever the merits of such a presumption when a large percentage of our population had access to a family farm, it is clearly refuted by modern conditions of ubiquitous private property, commodification, urbanization, and marketization. In today's urban-based market societies, the overwhelming majority of people must meet their own and their family's needs out of what they earn in the labor market. In the event that their earnings are low or uncertain, these needs must be met by some other means. If they or their relatives have savings, the problem may be postponed. If they cannot draw upon such savings, the social costs associated with their survival may be shouldered by private or public charity. Another possibility is that these costs may not be met. In either of the last two cases, a person's inability to cover the basic needs of themselves and their family generates a social cost with important, lasting, and undesirable consequences (Prasch, 2005).

Underlying the received theory of "free exchange" and "the workings of the market" is the proposition that everyone is participating because they believe they will improve their situation. It is trivial, but seems to be routinely overlooked, that for this assumption to be meaningful, people must have substantial and viable options (Prasch, 2006). However, it is immediately evident that options of this sort are not always present. Moreover, most of us have neither a trust fund nor a family farm to "fall back" on in the event that our wages are inadequate to support ourselves and our dependents. Lecture V proposes that when a substantial portion of the labor market is in such a position, their collective effort to cover the cost of their subsistence may set in motion forces that lead into a "poverty trap."

Labor, as was argued, is qualitatively different from other commodities. Most people cannot "substitute" out of the world of paid work. If their wages are below what is required to sustain themselves and their families as functioning economic and social entities, then our market economy has failed them. The morale and ability of the workforce will inevitably be reduced. Sooner or later, this will have implications for the quality of life in our society, and even the viability of our democracy. Moreover, we will have failed in the ethical sense when we allow some of our fellow citizens to become immisserated despite their willingness and capacity to earn a living by their own labor (Prasch and Sheth, 1999).

Third, when market prices depend heavily upon expectations, the stability of the market system is, and must be, an important consideration. Expectations, when they converge on the idea that an asset is overvalued and should be sold, can become self-fulfilling and self-reinforcing as more and more people rush to sell before everyone else. Under the correct conditions, especially in instances where the asset in question is being used as security for loans, widely and rapidly revised expectations can induce a catastrophic decline in asset prices. Hard experience has repeatedly demonstrated that such problems are most cheaply and efficiently addressed before they begin. Enforceable rules and checks on lending, greater transparency, the control of fraud, and a credible lender of last resort are each important, if only partial, solutions that have emerged to address the issues summarized above. Moreover, sound regulation has the potential to overcome another disturbing trend that has emerged with the deregulation of the market economy – an increasing divorce of risk from reward (Prasch, 2004a). None of these are problems that will disappear through denial or further deregulation.

All regulations, whatever their merits when enacted, must be constantly reevaluated and updated because financial market innovations and new technologies often undermine them, rendering them less effective. But whatever instruments of management and control are selected, clear thinking on the subject of financial regulation can only begin by forthrightly and unapologetically rejecting the now-widespread assumption that what is good for Wall Street is *ipso facto* good for Main Street. This presumption has caused tremendous harm to the American economy, and must be discarded if clear thinking and workable policies are to reemerge.

Fourth, there are instances in which the market works smoothly and efficiently, but we nevertheless experience what my Middlebury colleague David Colander calls a "failure of the market" (Colander, 2003). These are instances where some service or product is being efficiently produced and sold yet, for any of a number of reasons, a reasonable and decent society would wish that they were not.

Examples include slavery, certain varieties of military-grade weapons, child pornography, and sundry dangerous or vicious products that have few if any safe or legitimate uses.

In each case these "products" are known to create substantial harm in the event that they become commodities. Despite the often-heard claim that the market is best positioned to decide issues of inclusion and exclusion, ethics and prudence still have a role to play. Of course, while the broader concerns are clear, the question of where and how to "draw the line" is neither a simple nor fixed issue. Moreover, such decisions will never be permanently resolved in a democratic polity with a range of views and changing technical capabilities. The banning of marijuana is an instance of such an ongoing dispute, as is the ownership of some varieties of guns, and the distribution and availability of several other items or services.

The point is that everyone who participates in a more-or-less democratic polity likely knows of some item or items that our society would be better off without. But it is equally likely that good and decent people will disagree on the list of items to be controlled or banned. (Might I suggest car alarms?) Nevertheless, a more forthright discussion of the limits of commodification, and the appropriate realm of the market, would provide us with the space to discuss the meaning of a good society, in addition to the proper role and place of ethical considerations in economic policy.

The several grounds for regulation surveyed here are merely suggestive. It should be obvious that an exhaustive and full argument has not been presented. By contrast, a proper analysis of a proposed regulation would require an understanding of the qualities and likely uses of the commodity in question, in addition to an understanding of the "ideal type" of market within which it is sold. Inevitably, such studies will uncover idiosyncratic issues, obstacles, and even objections – including the costs of monitoring and administration – that may work for or against any particular prohibition or regulation.

But enough has been said to support our primary result which is that markets are more varied than might be inferred if we exclusively studied them through the lens of what I have termed "commodity" markets. By drawing upon the wrong "ideal type" of market to study a given sector of the economy, grievous and avoidable policy errors have occurred and even reoccurred. Policies enacted on such inaccurate premises have been flawed in ways that could have been anticipated with a more considered analytical framework, one that was open to the proposition that our economy features several varieties of markets. An additional concern is, of course, that some of these errors and false generalizations have come to be mainstays of economics textbooks and classroom instruction in economics. Hopefully, by starting with a more complete exposition of the theoretical foundations of economics, readers will develop a more sophisticated insight into the markets of the "real world."

The current political trend, one that insists that all values are or should be market values, and for this reason everything is or should be commodified, is both unenlightened and vicious. It stifles serious discussion and too often facilitates the adoption of policies that harm the economy, the nation, and international economic relations. The world's poor, the environment, and increasingly the world's middle classes, have each borne the burden of the policies that flow from these ideas. Most thinking people now understand that such policies are unsustainable, and that our conceptions and outlook must be modified in some fundamental ways. Important vested interests will tell us, as they ever have, that nothing can be done and that there is no alternative to the *status quo*. Ideally these lectures will prepare readers for the debates to come by leaving them with a greater degree of confidence in their understanding of how a market economy operates, and by affirming their belief that "Another world is possible."

Bibliography

Akerlof, George (1982), "Labor contracts as partial gift exchange", *Quarterly Journal of Economics*, **97** (4) (November), 543–69.

American Institute of Banking (1940), *Commercial Law*, New York.

Andrews, Marcellus (1999), *The Political Economy of Hope and Fear: Capitalism and the Black Condition in America*, New York: New York University Press.

Appadurai, Arjun (1986), "Introduction: commodities and the politics of value", in Arjun Appadurai (ed.), *The Social Life of Things: Commodities in Cultural Perspective*, New York: Cambridge University Press, chapter 1.

Arestis, Philip (1992), *The Post-Keynesian Approach to Economics*, Aldershot, UK and Brookfield, USA: Edward Elgar.

Axelrod, Robert (1984), *The Evolution of Cooperation*, New York: Basic Books.

Baker, Dean (2007), *The United States Since 1980*, New York: Cambridge University Press.

Bales, Kevin (1999), *Disposable People: New Slavery in the Global Economy*, Berkeley, CA: University of California Press.

Barro, Robert J. and Herschel I. Grossman (1971), "A general disequilibrium model of income and employment", *American Economic Review*, **61** (1) (March), 82–93.

Becker, Carl and George Stigler (1977), "De gustibus non est disputandum", *American Economic Review*, **67** (2) (March), 76–90.

Becker, Gary (1968), "Discrimination, economic", in David Sills (ed.), *International Encyclopedia of the Social Sciences*, vol. 4, New York: Macmillan, pp. 208–10.

Becker, Gary (1971), *The Economics of Discrimination*, 2nd edn, Chicago: University of Chicago Press.

Bergmann, Barbara (1974), "Occupational segregation, wages and profits when employers discriminate by race or sex", *Eastern Economic Journal*, **1** (2) (April/July), 103–10.

Bergmann, Barbara (1996), *In Defense of Affirmative Action*, New York: Basic Books.

Berlin, Isaiah (1969), *Four Essays on Liberty*, New York: Oxford University Press.

Bernays, Edward (1928), *Propaganda*, reprinted 2004, Brooklyn, NY: Ig Publishing.

Bernstein, Michael (2001), *A Perilous Progress: Economists and Public Purpose in Twentieth Century America*, Princeton, NJ: Princeton University Press.

Bluestone, Barry and Stephen Rose (1998), "The unmeasured labor force: the growth in work hours", Jerome Levy Institute public policy brief no. 39, Annandale-on-Hudson, NY.

Bourgois, Philippe (1995), *In Search of Respect: Selling Crack in El Barrio*, New York: Cambridge University Press.

Bowles, Samuel (1985), "The production process in a competitive economy: Walrasian, neo-Hobbesian, and Marxian models", *American Economic Review*, **75** (1) (March), 16–36.

Brosnan, Peter and Frank Wilkinson (1988), "A national statutory minimum wage and economic efficiency", *Contributions to Political Economy*, **7**, 1–48.

Card, David and Alan Krueger (1995), *Myth and Measurement: The New Economics of the Minimum Wage*, Princeton, NJ: Princeton University Press.

Cardozo, Benjamin (1922), *The Nature of the Judicial Process*, New Haven, CT: Yale University Press.

Carter, Thomas (1998), "Policy in a two-sector efficiency wage model: substituting good jobs for bad", *Journal of Post Keynesian Economics*, **20** (3) (Spring), 445–61.

Cassidy, John (2002), *Dot.con: The Greatest Story Ever Sold*, New York: HarperCollins.

Chandler, Alfred D. (1977), *The Visible Hand: The Managerial Revolution in American Business*, Cambridge, MA: Harvard University Press.

Chang, Ruth (ed.) (1997), *Incommensurability, Incomparability, and Practical Reason*, Cambridge, MA: Harvard University Press.

Clarke, Peter (1988), *The Keynesian Revolution in the Making, 1924–1936*, New York: Oxford University Press.

Clower, Robert (1965), "The Keynesian counter-revolution: a theoretical appraisal", in F.H. Hahn and R.P.R. Brechling (eds), *The Theory of Interest Rates*, London: Macmillan.

Colander, David (2003), "Integrating sex and drugs into the

principles course: market-failures versus failures-of-market outcomes", *Journal of Economic Education*, (Winter), 82–91.

Colander, David, Robert E. Prasch and Falguni A. Sheth (eds) (2004), *Race, Liberalism and Economics*, Ann Arbor, MI: University of Michigan Press.

Commons, John ([1893] 1963), *The Distribution of Wealth*, New York: Kelley Reprints.

Commons, John (1924), *Legal Foundations of Capitalism*, reprinted 1995, New Brunswick, NJ: Transaction Publishers.

Commons, John and John Andrews (1916), *Principles of Labor Legislation*, New York: Harper & Brothers.

Crotty, James and Gerald Epstein (1996), "In defense of capital controls", *Socialist Register*, **32**.

Davidson, Paul (1997), "Are grains of sand in the wheels of international finance sufficient to do the job when boulders are often required?", *Economic Journal*, **107** (442) (May), 671–86.

Dawson, Michael (2005), *The Consumer Trap: Big Business Marketing in American Life*, Champaign, IL: University of Illinois Press.

De Grauwe, Paul (1989), *International Money: Post-War Trends and Theories*, New York: Oxford University Press.

Dessing, Maryke (1999), "Implications for minimum wage policies of an S-shaped labor supply curve", manuscript in possession of author, International Center for Trade and Sustainable Development, Geneva.

Douglas, Mary (1992), "Why do people want goods?", in Shaun Hargreaves Heap and Angus Ross (eds), *Understanding the Enterprise Culture: Themes in the Work of Mary Douglas*, Edinburgh: Edinburgh University Press, chapter 2.

D'Souza, Dinesh (1995), *The End of Racism: Principles for a Multiracial Society*, New York: Free Press.

Dugger, William M. (1989), "Instituted process and enabling myth: the two faces of the market", *Journal of Economic Issues*, **23** (2) (June), 607–15.

Dunlop, John T. (1957), *The Theory of Wage Determination*, London: Macmillan.

Edwards, Richard, Michael Reich and David M. Gordon (eds) (1975), *Labor Market Segmentation*, Lexington, MA: D.C. Heath.

Eichengreen, Barry (1992), *Golden Fetters: The Gold Standard and the Great Depression, 1919–1939*, New York: Oxford University Press.

Eichengreen, Barry and Charles Wyplosz (1996), "Taxing international financial transactions to enhance the operation of the international monetary system", in Mahbub ul Haq, Inge Kaul and Isabelle Grunberg (eds), *The Tobin Tax: Coping with Financial Volatility*, New York: Oxford University Press.

Eichner, Alfred S. (1985), *Toward a New Economics: Essays in Post-Keynesian and Institutionalist Theory*, Armonk, NY: M.E. Sharpe.

Ellerman, David (1990), "The corporation as a democratic social institution", in Mark A. Lutz (ed.), *Social Economics: Retrospect and Prospect*, Boston, MA: Kluwer, chapter 11.

Ellerman, David (1992), *Property and Contract in Economics*, Cambridge, MA: Blackwell.

Ely, Richard T. (1914), *Property and Contract in Their Relations to the Distribution of Wealth*, New York: Macmillan.

Ely, Richard T., Thomas S. Adams, Max O. Lorenz and Allyn A. Young (1914), *Outlines of Economics*, revised edn, New York: Macmillan.

Erturk, Korkut (2006), "On the Tobin tax", *Review of Political Economy*, **18** (1) (January), 71–8.

Figart, Deborah, Ellen Mutari and Marilyn Power (2002), *Living Wages, Equal Wages: Gender and Labor Market Policies in the United States*, New York: Routledge.

Fine, Ben (1998), *Labour Market Theory: A Constructive Reassessment*, New York: Routledge.

Frank, Thomas (2000), *One Market Under God: Extreme Capitalism, Market Populism, and the End of Economic Democracy*, New York: Random House.

Frankel, Jeffrey (1996), "How well do markets work: might a Tobin tax help?", in Mahbub ul Haq, Inge Kaul and Isabelle Grunberg (eds), *The Tobin Tax: Coping with Financial Volatility*, New York: Oxford University Press.

Frankfurt, H.G. (1971), "Freedom of the will and the concept of a person", *Journal of Philosophy*, **68** (1) (January), 5–20.

Friedman, Milton (1953), *Essays in Positive Economics*, Chicago: University of Chicago Press.

Friedman, Milton (1962), *Capitalism and Freedom*, Chicago: University of Chicago Press.

Galbraith, James K. (2007), "Predation from Veblen till now", remarks to the Veblen Sesquicentennial Conference, Vadres, Norway.

Garegnani, Pierangelo (1990), "Quantity of capital", in John

Eatwell, Murray Milgate and Peter Newman (eds), *The New Palgrave: Capital Theory*, New York: Norton.

Ghosh, Atish (1995), "International capital mobility amongst the major industrialized countries: too little or too much", *Economic Journal*, **105** (January), 107–28.

Glickman, Lawrence B. (1997), *A Living Wage: American Workers and the Making of Consumer Society*, Ithaca, NY: Cornell University Press.

Goffman, Erving (1959), *The Presentation of Self in Everyday Life*, Garden City, NY: Doubleday Anchor Books.

Goldberger, Arthur S. and Charles F. Manski (1995), "Review article: the Bell curve by Herrnstein and Murray", *Journal of Economic Literature*, **33** (2) (June), 762–76.

Gordon, David M. (1996), *Fat and Mean: The Corporate Squeeze of Working Americans and the Myth of Managerial "Downsizing"*, New York: Free Press.

Gordon, David M., Richard Edwards and Michael Reich (1982), *Segmented Work, Divided Workers: The Historical Transformation of Labor in the United States*, New York: Cambridge University Press.

Graves Jr., Joseph L. (2001), *The Emperor's New Clothes: Biological Theories of Race at the Millennium*, New Brunswick, NJ.: Rutgers University Press.

Green, Thomas Hill (1881), "Liberal legislation and freedom of contract", reprinted 1986 in Paul Harris and John Morrow (eds), *T.H. Green: Lectures on the Principles of Political Obligation and Other Writings*, New York: Cambridge University Press.

Halberstam, David (1994), *October 1964*, New York: Random House.

Haq, Mahbub ul, Inge Kaul and Isabelle Grunberg (eds) (1996), *The Tobin Tax: Coping with Financial Volatility*, New York: Oxford University Press.

Harcourt, G.C. (1972), *Some Cambridge Controversies in the Theory of Capital*, Cambridge: Cambridge University Press.

Harrison, Bennett and Andrew Sum (1979), "The theory of 'dual' or segmented labor markets", *Journal of Economic Issues*, **13** (3) (September), 687–706.

Harvey, John T. (1993), "Daily exchange rate variance", *Journal of Post Keynesian Economics*, **15** (4) (Summer), 515–40.

Hayek, Friedrich von (1945), "The use of knowledge in economics", *American Economic Review*, **35** (4) (September), 519–30.

Hegel, G.W.F. (1976), *Philosophy of Right*, translated by T.M. Knox, New York: Oxford University Press.

Herrnstein, Richard J. and Charles Murray (1994), *The Bell Curve: Intelligence and Class Structure in American Life*, New York: Free Press.

Hicks, John R. (1939), *Value and Capital*, Oxford: Clarendon Press.

Hirschman, Albert O. (1991), *The Rhetoric of Reaction: Perversity, Futility, Jeopardy*, Cambridge, MA: Harvard University Press.

Hobhouse, L.T. ([1911] 1994), *Liberalism and Other Writings*, New York: Cambridge University Press.

Hockstader, Lee (2004), "Involuntary reenlistments: to prevent troop shortages, the Army blocks some departures", *Washington Post National Weekly Edition*, (5–11 January), 29.

Hodgson, Geoffrey M. (2003), "The hidden persuaders: institutions and individuals in economic theory", *Cambridge Journal of Economics*, **27** (2) (March), 159–75.

Holmes, Stephen (1997), "What Russia teaches us now: how weak states threaten freedom", *American Prospect*, **33** (July-August), 30–39.

Hovenkamp, Herbert (1988), "Labor conspiracies in American law, 1880–1930", *Texas Law Review*, **66**, 919–65.

Katz, Michael L. and Harvey Rosen (1991), *Microeconomics*, Boston, MA: Irwin.

Kaufman, Bruce E. (1993), *The Origins and Evolution of the Field of Industrial Relations*, Ithaca, NY: Cornell University Press.

Kaufman, Bruce E. (1994), *The Economics of Labor Markets*, 4th edn, New York: Dryden.

Keynes, John Maynard (1964), *The General Theory of Employment, Interest and Money*, first printed 1936, New York: Harcourt, Brace.

Kindleberger, Charles. P. (1996), *Manias, Panics and Crashes*, 3rd edn, New York: John Wiley.

Krueger, Anne O. (1963), "The economics of discrimination", *Journal of Political Economy*, **71** (5) (October), 481–6.

Kurz, Heinz (1990), "Debates in capital theory", in John Eatwell, Murray Milgate and Peter Newman (eds), *The New Palgrave: Capital Theory*, New York: Norton.

Landler, Mark (2004), "German court convicts Internet cannibal of manslaughter", *New York Times*, (January 31).

Lavoie, Marc (1992), *Foundations of Post-Keynesian Economic Analysis*, Aldershot, UK and Brookfield, US: Edward Elgar.

Law, Marc T. (2003), "The origins of state pure food regulation", *Journal of Economic History*, **63** (4) (December), 1103–30.

Law, Marc T. and Sukkoo Kim (2005), "Specialization and regulation: the rise of professionals and the emergence of occupational licensing regulation", *Journal of Economic History*, **65** (3), 723–56.

Lazonick, William (1991), *Business Organization and the Myth of the Market Economy*, New York: Cambridge University Press.

Lazonick, William and Mary O'Sullivan (2000), "Maximizing shareholder value: a new ideology of corporate governance", *Economy and Society*, **29** (1), 13–35.

Leibenstein, Harvey (1950), "Bandwagon, snob, and Veblen effects in the theory of consumers' demand", *Quarterly Journal of Economics*, **64** (2) (May), 183–207.

Leijonhufvud, Axel (1981), *Information and Coordination: Essays in Macroeconomic Theory*, New York: Oxford University Press.

Lessing, Lawrence (2001), "Jail time in the digital age", *New York Times* Op-Ed section, (July 30), p. A21.

Lessing, Lawrence (2004), *Free Culture: How Big Media Uses Technology and the Law to Lock Down Culture and Control Creativity*, New York: Penguin.

Lester, Richard A. (1941), *Economics of Labor*, New York: Macmillan.

Lester, Richard A. (1947), "Marginalism, minimum wages, and labor markets", *American Economic Review*, **37** (March), 135–48.

Levin-Waldman, Oren (2000), "Minimum wage and justice?", *Review of Social Economy*, **58** (1) (March), 43–62.

Levin-Waldman, Oren (2001), *The Case of the Minimum Wage: Competing Policy Models*, Albany, NY: SUNY Press.

Levine, David P. (1988), *Needs, Rights, and the Market*, Boulder, CO: Lynne Rienner.

Levine, David P. (1995), *Wealth and Freedom: An Introduction to Political Economy*, New York: Cambridge University Press.

Levine, Robert (1997), *A Geography of Time*, New York: Basic Books.

Linder, Marc (2002), *The Autocratically Flexible Workplace: A History of Overtime Regulation in the United States*, Iowa City, IA: Fãnpìhuà Press.

Litwack, Leon F. (1998), *Trouble in Mind: Black Southerners in the Age of Jim Crow*, New York: Alfred A. Knopf.

Llewellyn, Karl N. (1931), "What price contract? An essay in perspective", *Yale Law Journal*, **40** (May), 704–51.

Loury, Glenn C. (1998), "Discrimination in the post-civil rights era: beyond market interactions", *Journal of Economic Perspectives*, **12** (2), 117–26.

Loury, Glenn C. (2002), *The Anatomy of Racial Inequality*, Cambridge, MA.: Harvard University Press.

Lutz, Mark (1999), *Economics for the Common Good: Two Centuries of Social Economic Thought in the Humanistic Tradition*, New York: Routledge.

Lutz, Mark and Kenneth Lux (1979), *The Challenge of Humanistic Economics*, Reading, MA: Benjamin Cummings.

Lynn, Barry (2006), "Breaking the chain: the antitrust case against Wal-Mart", *Harper's Magazine*, (July), 29–36.

Macaulay, S. (1963), "Non-contractual relations in business", *American Sociological Review*, **28**, 55–70.

MacKay, Charles ([1852] 1980), *Extraordinary Popular Delusions and the Madness of Crowds*, 2nd edn, New York: Harmony.

MacNeil, Ian (1974), "The many futures of contracts", *Southern California Law Review*, **47**, 691–816.

MacNeil, Ian (1978), "Contracts: adjustments of long-term economic relations under classical, neoclassical, and relational contract law", *Northwestern University Law Review*, **72**, 854–906.

Maloney, Thomas N. and Warren C. Whatley (1995), "Making the effort: the contours of racial discrimination in Detroit's labor markets, 1920–1940", *Journal of Economic History*, **55** (3) (September), 465–93.

Marshall, Alfred (1920), *Principles of Economics*, 8th edn, reprinted 1997, Amherst, NY: Prometheus Books.

Milgrom, Paul R., Douglass C. North and Barry R. Weingast (1990), "The role of institutions in the revival of trade: the law merchant, private judges, and the Champagne fairs", *Economics and Politics*, **2** (1) (March), 1–23.

Mill, John Stuart (1859), *On Liberty*, reprinted 1985, London: Penguin Classics.

Mill, John Stuart (1904), *Principles of Political Economy with Some of Their Applications to Social Philosophy*, 5th edn, New York: D. Appleton and Company.

Mincer, Jacob (1963), "Market prices, opportunity costs, and income effects", in Carl Christ, Milton Friedman, Leo Goodman, Zvi Griliches, Arnold Harberger, Nissan Liviatan, Jacob Mincer, Yair Mundlak, Marc Nerlove, Don Patinkin, Lester Telser and Henri

Theil (eds), *Measurement in Economics: Studies in Mathematical Economics and Econometrics in Memory of Yehuda Grunfeld*, Stanford, CA: Stanford University Press.

Minsky, Hyman P. (1986), *Stabilizing an Unstable Economy*, New Haven, CT: Yale University Press.

Mishel, Lawrence, Jared Bernstein and John Schmitt (1999), *The State of Working America 1998–1999*, Ithaca, NY: Cornell University Press.

Morgenstern, Oscar (1940), "Demand theory reconsidered", *Quarterly Journal of Economics*, **62** (2) (February), 165–201.

Morgenstern, Oscar (1963), *On the Accuracy of Economic Observations*, Princeton, NJ: Princeton University Press.

Nordlund, Willis J. (1997), *The Quest for a Living Wage: The History of the Federal Minimum Wage Program*, Westport, CT: Greenwood Press.

North, Douglass C. (1990), *Institutions, Institutional Change and Economic Performance*, New York: Cambridge University Press.

Nozick, Robert (1974), *Anarchy, State and Utopia*, New York: Basic Books.

Nussbaum, Martha C. (2000), "The future of feminist liberalism", *Proceedings and Addresses of the American Philosophical Association*, **74** (2) (November), 47–79.

Nussbaum, Martha C. (2001), "The costs of tragedy: some moral limits of cost-benefit analysis", in Matthew D. Adler and Eric A. Posner (eds), *Cost-Benefit Analysis: Economic, Philosophical, and Legal Perspectives*, Chicago: University of Chicago Press, pp. 169–200.

Paulsen, George E. (1996), *A Living Wage for the Forgotten Man: The Quest for Fair Labor Standards, 1933–1941*, Selinsgrove, PA: Susquehanna University Press.

Pollin, Robert, Dean Baker and Marc Schaberg (2003), "Securities transactions taxes for U.S. financial markets", *Eastern Economic Journal*, **29** (4), 527–58.

Pound, Roscoe (1909), "Liberty of contract", *Yale Law Journal*, **17** (7) (May), 454–87.

Pound, Roscoe (1922), *An Introduction to the Philosophy of Law*, reprinted 1982, New Haven, CT: Yale University Press.

Prasch, Robert E. (1992), "Economics and merger mania: a critique of efficient markets theory", *Journal of Economic Issues*, **26** (2) (June), 635–43.

Prasch, Robert E. (1996), "In defense of the minimum wage", *Journal of Economic Issues*, **30** (2) (June), 391–7.

Prasch, Robert E. (1997), "The overburdened consumer: the economics of technological change in the service sector", working paper, Department of Economics, Vassar College.

Prasch, Robert E. (1998a), "Complexity and economic method: an institutionalist perspective", in David Colander (ed.), *Complexity and the History of Economic Thought*, New York: Routledge.

Prasch, Robert E. (1998b), "American economists and minimum wage legislation during the progressive era: 1912–1923", *Journal of the History of Economic Thought*, **20** (2) (June), 161–75.

Prasch, Robert E. (1998c), "Review of *The Winner-Take-All Society*" by Robert H. Frank and Philip J. Cook", *Eastern Economic Journal*, **24** (2) (Spring), 244–6.

Prasch, Robert E. (1999), "American economists in the progressive era on the minimum wage", *Journal of Economic Perspectives*, **13** (2) (Spring), 221–30.

Prasch, Robert E. (2000a), "Integrating complexity into the principles of macroeconomics", Ch. 11 in David Colander (ed.), *The Complexity Vision and the Teaching of Economics*, Cheltenham, UK and Northampton, MA, USA: Edward Elgar.

Prasch, Robert E. (2000b), "Revising the labor supply curve: implications for work time and minimum wage legislation", Ch. 10 in Lonnie Golden and Deborah M. Figart (eds), *Working Time: International Trends, Theory and Policy Perspectives*, New York: Routledge.

Prasch, Robert E. (2000c), "John Bates Clark's defense of mandatory arbitration and minimum wage legislation", *Journal of the History of Economic Thought*, **22** (2) (June), 251–63.

Prasch, Robert E. (2003), "Technical change, competition, and the poor", *Journal of Economic Issues*, **37** (2) (June), 479–85.

Prasch, Robert E. (2004a), "Shifting risk: the divorce of risk from reward in American capitalism", *Journal of Economic Issues*, **38** (2) (June), 405–12.

Prasch, Robert E. (2004b), "How is labor distinct from broccoli? Some unique characteristics of labor and their importance for economic analysis and policy", Ch. 8 in Janet Knoedler and Dell Champlin (eds), *The Institutionalist Tradition in Labor Economics*, Armonk, NY: M.E. Sharpe.

Prasch, Robert E. (2005), "The social cost of labor", *Journal of Economic Issues*, **39** (2) (June), 439–45.

Prasch, Robert E. (2006), " 'Free entry and exit' from the market: simplifying or substantive assumption?", *Journal of Economic Issues*, **40** (2) (June), 317–24.

Prasch, Robert E. (2007), "Professor Lester and the neoclassicals: the 'marginalist controversy' and the postwar academic debate over minimum wage legislation: 1945–1950", *Journal of Economic Issues*, **41** (3) (September), 809–25.

Prasch, Robert E. and Falguni A. Sheth (1999), "The economics and ethics of minimum wage legislation", *Review of Social Economy*, **57** (Winter), 466–87.

Purdy, Jedediah S. (1998), "The Chicago acid bath: the impoverished logic of 'law and economics' ", *American Prospect*, **36** (January–February), 88–95.

Radin, Margaret Jane (1996), *Contested Commodities: The Trouble with Trade in Sex, Children, Body Parts, and Other Things*, Cambridge, MA: Harvard University Press.

Ransom, Roger, and Richard Sutch (1977), *One Kind of Freedom: The Economic Consequences of Emancipation*, New York: Cambridge University Press.

Reichheld, Frederick F. (1993), "Loyalty-based management", *Harvard Business Review*, **71** (2) (March–April), 64–73.

Reichheld, Frederick F. and W. Earl Sasser, Jr. (1990), "Zero defections: quality comes to services", *Harvard Business Review*, **68** (5) (September–October), 105–11.

Rose, Carol M. (1988), "Crystals and mud in property law", *Stanford Law Review*, **40** (February), 577–610.

Ryan, John A. (1919), *Distributive Justice: The Right and Wrong of our Present Distribution of Wealth*, New York: Macmillan.

Schor, Juliet B. (1992), *The Overworked American: The Unexpected Decline of Leisure*, New York: Basic Books.

Schwab, Stewart (1986), "Is statistical discrimination efficient?", *American Economic Review*, (March), 228–34.

Seager, Henry Rogers (1913), "The theory of the minimum wage", *American Labor Legislation Review*, **3**, 81–91.

Sen, Amartya (1999), *Development as Freedom*, New York: Alfred A. Knopf.

Sennett, Richard (2003), *Respect: In a World of Inequality*, New York: Norton.

Shapiro, Carl and Joseph E. Stiglitz (1984), "Equilibrium unemployment as a worker discipline device", *American Economic Review*, **74** (3) (June), 433–44.

Sharif, Mohammed (2003), "A behavioural analysis of the subsistence standard of living", *Cambridge Journal of Economics*, **27**, 191–207.

Smith, Adam (1776), *An Inquiry into the Nature and Causes of the Wealth of Nations*, reprinted 1937, New York: Modern Library.

Sowell, Thomas (1981a), *Markets and Minorities*, New York: Basic Books.

Sowell, Thomas (1981b), *Ethnic America*, New York: Basic Books.

Sraffa, Piero (1926), "The laws of returns under competitive conditions", *Economic Journal*, **36** (December), 535–50.

Steele, Shelby (1990), *The Content of Our Character*, New York: St. Martin's Press.

Steinfeld, Robert J. (2001), *Coercion, Contract, and Free Labor in the Nineteenth Century*, New York: Cambridge University Press.

Stigler, George (1946), "The economics of minimum wage legislation", *American Economic Review*, **36** (3) (June), 358–65.

Stigler, George (1982), *The Economist as Preacher, and Other Essays*, Chicago: University of Chicago Press.

Stiglitz, Joseph (1987), "The causes and consequences of the dependence of quality on price", *Journal of Economic Literature*, **25** (1) (March), 1–48.

Stiglitz, Joseph (2002), *Globalization and Its Discontents*, New York: Norton.

Stiglitz, Joseph (2004), *The Roaring Nineties: A New History of the World's Most Prosperous Decade*, New York: Norton.

Stiglitz, Joseph E. and Andrew Weiss (1981), "Credit rationing in markets with imperfect information", *American Economic Review*, **71** (3) (June), 393–410.

Styron, William (1979), *Sophie's Choice*, New York: Random House.

Taylor, George W. (1957), "An evaluation of wage theory", in George W. Taylor and Frank C. Pierson (eds), *New Concepts in Wage Determination*, New York: McGraw-Hill, pp. 3–31.

Taylor, John B. (1998), *Economics*, 2nd edn, New York: Houghton Mifflin.

Thurow, Lester (1969), *Poverty and Discrimination*, Washington, DC: Brookings Institution.

Tobin, James (1978), "A proposal for international monetary reform", *Eastern Economic Journal*, **4** (July-October), 153–9.

Veblen, Thorstein (1899), *The Theory of the Leisure Class: An Economic Study of Institutions*, reprinted 1998, Amherst, NY: Prometheus Books.

Veblen, Thorstein (1904), *The Theory of Business Enterprise*, reprinted 1978, New Brunswick, NJ: Transaction Publishers.

Waltman, Jerold (2000), *The Politics of the Minimum Wage*, Champaign, IL: University of Illinois Press.

Weisbrot, Mark, Dean Baker, Egor Kraev and Judy Chen (2001), *The Scorecard on Globalization 1980–2000: 20 Years of Diminished Progress*, Washington, DC: Center for Economic and Policy Research.

Welch, Finis (1973), "Black-white differences in returns to schooling", *American Economic Review*, **63** (5) (December), 893–907.

Index